KRITHI KODE

Art of Perception

A daughter's guide to living, think better live better

"Perception creates reality"
K.K

Contents

Acknowledgments — iv

Introduction — 1

I   Part one

1   Art of Perception — 5

2   Identity — 8

3   Go Beyond Borders — 15

4   Dream Big — 19

5   Law of Manifestation — 27

6   Be Bold — 32

7   Be Strong — 37

Self Confidence — 39

8   Be a Thinker and a Tinkerer — 42

9   Wealth and Abundance — 46

Greed and ambition — 51

Flow of Money — 55

Being Humble — 58

Pride vs Confidence — 59

Success — 61

10 Embrace Failure — 64

II   Part Two

11 Self Love   73
12 Live Freely   83
    Love Freely   87
    Unconditional Love   91
13 Emotional Vulnerability   94
14 Two Sides of The Coin   101
15 Yin and Yang   106
    Karma   108
16 The Art of Empathy   110
    The Art of Compassion   117
17 The Art of Humility   122
18 The Art of Giving   127
    Giver vs Receiver   131

III Part Three

19 Living in the Moment   137
    The Art of Contentment   140
20 The Best Place in Life   144
21 Time   149
    Time Helps us Grow   150
    Time Heals   153
22 Journey of Life   156
    Life is a Journey not a Competition   158
    Embrace the End   161
23 Swadharma   163
24 Self-Reflection   174

Appendix   178

Acknowledgments

I'm incredibly grateful to the amazing people who have guided and inspired me throughout this journey. This book wouldn't have been possible without their wisdom and support.

First and foremost, I want to say thank you to my dad, Krishnna Kode. Your wisdom and guidance have been the foundation of everything I've learned and written about. The way you've navigated life and shared your understanding with me is truly inspiring. I've always admired your ability to see and explain the world in such a thoughtful way, and I'm so grateful that you've passed that down to me.

I also want to extend a heartfelt thank you to my grandma, Aruna Kumari Kode. Your unwavering love and encouragement have been a constant source of comfort and strength. Your support has given me the confidence to explore and share my own perspectives.

A special thanks to my Uncle Dr. Ravi Babu Kode and my late Grandfather Dr. Subhas Babu Kode. The profound wisdom and life lessons you've shared with my dad have had a lasting impact on both him and me. Your experiences and insights have helped shape his understanding of life, and through him, they've reached me as well.

Although my grandfather passed away at the young age of 38, when my dad was just 10 years old. During their limited time together, my grandfather imparted invaluable lessons to my dad, which is how I've come to know him, despite never having met him myself.

Ravi Uncle served as a father figure to my dad following the death of my grandfather especially between the ages of 17 and 25. He helped to fill the paternal void that my dad experienced, providing him with a foundation of wisdom and a deep understanding of life and the importance of self-reflection.

Each of you has played a crucial role in my growth and in the creation of this book. Your guidance and support means more to me than words can express. Thank you for being my mentors, my inspirations, and my sources of strength.

To each of you, thank you for the invaluable lessons and the unwavering support. This book is as much yours as it is mine.

With all my love and gratitude,

Krithi Kode

Introduction

As I sit down to write this introduction, I find myself reflecting on how this book came to be and what it means to me. I'm just 18 years old, and I don't pretend to have all the answers. In fact, the beauty of this journey is that I'm still learning, growing, and discovering new perspectives every day. This book, "Art of Perception," is a collection of insights and ideas that have shaped my life, and it's my hope that by sharing them, I can become a companion in your own journey.

Growing up, I was fortunate enough to have a teacher and mentor who was also my best friend—my dad. From the earliest days of my life, he's been guiding me through the complex and often confusing landscape of human experience. Through countless conversations and shared moments, he's helped me see the world through different lenses. Whether it was understanding empathy, exploring the depths of identity, or embracing the beauty of unconditional love, his wisdom has been a constant source of light.

This book is a reflection of the lessons I've learned from him and the growth I've experienced along the way. It's a snapshot of my evolving perspective on various aspects of life, from emotional vulnerability and the art of giving to the value of time and the importance of living in the present moment. Each chapter is an exploration of how shifting our perceptions can profoundly impact our lives.

I want to be clear about something: I'm not here to preach or present myself as an expert. I'm just an ordinary person sharing what I've discovered, and I'm still figuring things out myself. The journey of writing this book has been as transformative as it has been enlightening. As I wrote each word, I found myself growing and gaining clarity on the topics I was exploring. The ideas and insights in these pages are a testament to my own growth and the continuous evolution of my understanding.

My hope is that by sharing these perspectives, you'll find something that resonates with you, something that sparks a new way of seeing the world. I'm not offering perfect answers or solutions—just a glimpse into my journey and the wisdom that has guided me so far.

Thank you for joining me on this adventure. Let's explore the art of perception together and see what new and wonderful perspectives we can discover along the way.

I

Part one

UNDERSTANDING YOURSELF

1

Art of Perception

"We don't see things as they are, we see them as we are"
Anais Nin

Perception is a fascinating concept that shapes our entire existence. It's like putting on a pair of glasses that filters how we interpret the world around us. Our perception forms our unique perspective, influencing how we see ourselves, others, and everything else. As the saying goes, "Yad bhavam tad bhavathi" - as you think, so you become.

The power of our thoughts in shaping our reality cannot be underestimated. Our perception impacts our emotions and influences the experiences we have in life. It even affects how we remember things and what we aspire to achieve. These desires then drive our actions, ultimately molding our character and guiding us towards our destined path.

Therefore, it is crucial for us to be aware of how our perception guides us through life. By understanding and managing our perceptions effectively, we can navigate towards the future we envision for ourselves.

One important thing to remember is that perception is not fixed; it can evolve and change over time as we learn and grow. This gives us immense power to shape our lives according to how we want them to be. By being mindful of our perceptions and actively seeking to broaden our understanding, we can navigate through life with greater clarity and purpose.

Imagine a person who sees every setback as an opportunity for growth instead of a roadblock. Their positive perception allows them to overcome challenges with resilience and determination. They view failure not as defeat but as stepping stones towards success.

On the other hand, someone with a negative perception might see every setback as confirmation of their inadequacy or unworthiness. Their self-doubt holds them back from taking risks or pursuing their dreams wholeheartedly.

Our perceptions also influence how we perceive others around us. A person with a judgmental mindset may quickly form biased opinions about people based on superficial factors such as appearance or background without truly getting to know them on a deeper level.

However, by actively working to broaden our understanding, we can challenge these preconceived notions and see people for who they truly are. By practicing empathy and compassion, we can foster meaningful connections and build a more inclusive and harmonious society.

But how do we actively manage our perceptions? It starts with self-awareness. We need to be conscious of our thoughts and how they shape our reality. When faced with a challenging situation or person, take a moment to pause and reflect on your initial perception. Is it colored by past experiences or biases? Are there alternative ways to interpret the situation?

By questioning our initial perceptions, we open ourselves up to new possibilities. This practice requires humility and an openness to growth. It may feel uncomfortable at first as it challenges long-held beliefs, but the rewards are immense.

Additionally, seeking diverse perspectives is crucial in expanding our own understanding. Engage in conversations with people from different backgrounds and listen attentively to their stories. By doing so, we gain insight into experiences beyond our own and cultivate empathy towards others.

Remember that perception is not just about how we see the world; it is also about how we see ourselves. Our self-perception influences our confidence levels, aspirations, and overall well-being.

Perception is a powerful force that shapes every aspect of our lives. By actively managing our perceptions through self-awareness, questioning biases, seeking diverse perspectives, and cultivating empathy towards others as well as ourselves; we can navigate through life with purposeful intention.

So let us embark on this journey of self-discovery together – one where we continuously explore the depths of perception's artistry while striving for personal growth and development along the way.

2

Identity

"To be yourself in a world that is constantly trying to make you something else is the greatest accomplishment"
Ralph Waldo Emerson

Have you ever stopped to think about how much of our lives are dictated by societal expectations and norms? We often find ourselves chasing after certain identities or lifestyles because we think that's what we're supposed to do. We go to college, get a job, buy a house, and start a family because that's what we're told is the "right" way to live. But what's to say that's the only right way?

When we take a step back and look at the bigger picture, we realize that these identities are just constructs created by society. They have nothing to do with our true selves. We don't have to fit into a specific mold or follow a certain path to be happy and fulfilled. True happiness lies in embracing our individuality and living life on our terms.

It's crazy when you think about it. We put so much effort into fitting into these predefined boxes of what a "normal" person is supposed to be like. We try to be what our parents, friends, and teachers want us to be. We try to fit into the mold of what society deems acceptable. And all the while, we're neglecting our true identity!

The truth is that the things we think define us are all just constructs of our minds. We're not just our job title, our hobbies, or our social status. We're so much more than that! Our true identity cannot be confined within societal boundaries.

It's time for us to break free from these limiting beliefs and start exploring who we truly are at the core of our being.

Let's focus on cultivating passions that set your soul on fire, and indulge in activities that bring you joy without worrying about fitting into someone else's idea of how we should be.

In this journey of self-discovery, don't be afraid to question everything you thought defined you. Challenge the beliefs that have held you back and prevented you from fully expressing your true essence.

Only when we let go of these preconceived notions can we truly find our authentic selves. Only then can we experience a sense of fulfillment and purpose in our lives. Remember that our identities are not fixed or static. We are ever-evolving beings, constantly growing and learning. Embrace change wholeheartedly, for it is through change that we discover new dimensions within ourselves.

Let go of the need to define ourselves so rigidly, for it limits our potential and inhibits our growth. Instead, let's focus on being present in the moment and living our lives authentically - without the constraints of labels or societal expectations.

Unmasking the illusion of identity allows us to tap into our true potential - a limitless wellspring of creativity, resilience, and joy. It is within this space that we can truly find purpose and live a life filled with meaning.

As we navigate through life, it is important to remember that our identity extends far beyond the limitations of societal categorizations. We often find ourselves boxed into certain roles and labels, whether it be our family, friends, or job titles. However, true fulfillment lies in transcending these boundaries and embracing all aspects of who we are.

We are so much more than just one aspect of our lives. Our identity is woven from the threads of our experiences, beliefs, and perspectives. It is a mosaic that reflects the depth and complexity of our being. To confine ourselves within narrow definitions would be to deny the richness that resides within us.

Unfortunately, society has a tendency to judge us based on superficial factors such as wealth, race, background, and appearance. People make assumptions about us before they even truly get to know us. This inclination to oversimplify stems from a natural human instinct to categorize and understand the world around us. However, we must resist succumbing to these judgments ourselves.

Let us take the time to truly see each other for who we are beyond these shallow labels and stereotypes. By doing so, we open doors for authentic connections and meaningful relationships. We break free from the constraints imposed upon us by societal expectations and create space for genuine understanding.

It is not uncommon to feel trapped by society's definition of success or beauty – particularly when it comes to money and appearance. From a young age, we are bombarded with messages that measure success solely by financial wealth or physical attractiveness. These narrow standards can leave us feeling inadequate or unfulfilled.

However, it is crucial to recognize that success comes in many forms – success can be found in pursuing passions with fervor; happiness can be achieved by staying true to oneself midst adversity; beauty radiates from within when authenticity shines through.

Our worth should never be defined solely by external factors such as bank accounts or qualifications. We need not conform to society's rigid expectations to find fulfillment. Instead, we should focus on embracing our unique qualities and allowing them to flourish.

By breaking free from the confines of societal norms, we open ourselves up to a world of endless possibilities. We have the power to shape our own destinies and create an identity that is true to ourselves. An identity that brings us happiness. We have different passions, wants, needs, ideas. Embrace your true self unapologetically and allow your authentic identity to shine brightly in this world.

Let us shed the limitations imposed upon us by others and embrace the vast expanse of our being. Let us celebrate every facet of who we are – from our achievements and passions to our flaws and vulnerabilities. By doing so, we take a massive step in the journey of self-discovery that will allow us to grow and accomplish more than we ever thought possible.

"You are what you believe yourself to be"
Paulo Coelho

As human beings, we often underestimate our own abilities and limit ourselves based on our perceived identity. We create boundaries around who we think we are and what we think we can achieve. However, these limitations are often self-imposed and prevent us from realizing our true potential.

It's time to break free from these self-imposed limitations and embrace the power of expanding our identities. You are totally capable of being that amazing person you've always dreamed of being. It's just a matter of shifting your mindset and believing in yourself.

Don't let anyone, including yourself, hold you back from reaching your full potential. Think big and don't limit yourself. Your identity is not set in stone; it can continue to grow and evolve over time.

* * *

Imagine a world where everyone fully embraces their true selves without fear or hesitation. A world where people break free from societal expectations or self-doubt to pursue their passions wholeheartedly. How amazing would that be.

When we expand our identities beyond what society dictates or what we've been conditioned to believe about ourselves, incredible things happen. We tap into hidden talents and strengths that were waiting to be unleashed.

So how do we begin this journey towards expanding our identities?

Firstly, it starts with recognizing that our current beliefs about ourselves may be limiting us. Take a moment to reflect on the self-imposed boundaries you have created and question their validity. Are they truly serving you, or are they holding you back?

Next, embrace the idea that your identity is not fixed. You are not limited to who you were yesterday or who you think you are today. Your identity is fluid and can expand as much as you allow it.

Now, it's time to explore new possibilities. Step outside of your comfort zone and try new things. Push yourself beyond what feels familiar and safe. Embrace challenges and setbacks as opportunities for growth.

Surround yourself with people who support and encourage your growth. Seek out mentors or role models who have expanded their identities and are already where you want to be. Learn from their experiences and let their stories inspire you.

My dad often reminded me, "Don't limit yourself to just one identity." He believed it was far more enriching to be a jack of all trades than to focus solely on mastering one thing. This perspective really resonated with me, especially as I navigated the complexities of adolescence and early adulthood. In a world that often pressures individuals especially teenagers to pigeonhole themselves into specific roles or career paths, his words served as a reminder that life is meant to be explored in all its multifaceted glory. Embracing diverse identities prevents life from feeling dull; it keeps things vibrant and engaging. Whether it was picking up a guitar, experimenting with painting, or dabbling in poetry, my dad encouraged me to push beyond my comfort zone. He wanted me to be a well-rounded individual, someone who could appreciate the beauty of various disciplines while also developing a rich tapestry of experiences and skills.

Additionally, he stressed the importance of being a creator rather than just a consumer. In an age where it's easy to fall into the trap of mindless consumption--scrolling through endless social media feeds or binge-watching shows--he urged me to take an active role in shaping my life and the world around me. He believed that everyone has the capacity to contribute something unique and valuable, and he wanted me to recognize that potential within myself.

This philosophy not only inspired me to pursue my interests

but also instilled a sense of responsibility to share my
voice and ideas with others. Whether through writing
stories, composing music, or simply engaging in
conversations that challenge the status quo, he encouraged
me to always bring something new into the world. His
guidance has shaped my understanding of identity as a fluid
concept, one that thrives on exploration, creativity, and
the courage to embrace the unknown.

Remember, expanding your identity is a continuous journey. It takes time, effort, and a willingness to step into the unknown.

As you expand your identity, don't forget to celebrate every milestone along the way. Acknowledge how far you've come while keeping sight of the limitless potential that lies ahead.

So go out there and be the best version of yourself! Expand your identity beyond what you thought was possible. Believe in yourself wholeheartedly because when you do, magic happens.

The world needs individuals like us – those who dare to dream big, believe in themselves unconditionally, and continuously expand their identities for the greater good.

So take that chance today; believe in yourself; see where it takes you – for within lies a world of endless possibilities waiting to become reality!

"Life is not only about finding yourself, life is about creating yourself"
George Bernard Shaw

3

Go Beyond Borders

"It takes courage to push yourself to places you have never
been before… to test your limits… to break through barriers.
And the day came when the risk it took to stay tight inside
the bud was more painful than the risk it took to blossom"
  Anais nin

In a world that often encourages conformity, it is time to break free
from the idea of letting our differences divide us, let's embrace
and celebrate what makes each of us special. Art of Perception
teaches us that embracing diversity, whether it be in cultures, beliefs,
or perspectives, is what truly makes our world a vibrant and beautiful
place. We should strive to understand, appreciate, and learn from one
another's unique experiences.

Each person brings their own set of experiences and knowledge to
the table. It is through this diversity that we can greatly enrich our
own lives. Rather than shying away from unfamiliar perspectives or
cultures, let us embrace them with open arms. By doing so, we can

expand our horizons, challenge our preconceived notions, and foster a deeper sense of empathy and understanding.

When we celebrate our differences instead of fearing them, we open ourselves up to a whole new world of possibilities and growth. Our differences are not barriers; they are bridges that connect us in ways we never imagined. By embracing diversity in all its forms – be it race, ethnicity, religion or gender – we give ourselves the chance to broaden our minds and truly enjoy life for what it is.

Let us not be afraid to celebrate our differences; they are what make us unique individuals. In celebrating diversity together as a society, we build an environment where everyone feels valued and respected for who they are – regardless of their background or beliefs.

Imagine a world where people come together not despite their differences but because of them. A world where there is no fear or discrimination based on race or religion but rather an appreciation for the richness each culture brings. Such a world is possible if each one of us takes responsibility for creating an inclusive society.

It starts with acknowledging that diversity is both natural and essential for progress. Just as different colors come together to create beautiful artwork on a canvas, so too can different cultures, beliefs, and perspectives come together to create a beautiful and harmonious society. Diversity is what makes our lives colorful and fun, instead of monotonous and boring.

In this celebration of diversity lies the power to break down barriers and build bridges – bridges that connect people from all walks of life. By reaching out across borders and boundaries, we can learn from one another and grow together. Our shared humanity becomes a unifying force that transcends any differences we may have.

Let us create an environment where diversity is not only accepted but cherished. Together, we can pave the way for a future where inclusivity reigns supreme – where every individual feels valued for who they are.

So let us go beyond borders – both physical and metaphorical – as we celebrate diversity in all its forms. It is through this celebration that we can build a more inclusive and harmonious society for generations to come.

My dad has always emphasized the value of diversity, instilling in me the belief that the world is rich from countless perspectives and experiences. He encouraged me to look beyond the conventional limits of my thinking, to challenge the norms that often go unquestioned. This journey towards embracing diversity is ongoing and multifaceted, filled with moments of reflection and growth. As I navigate through various experiences, I recognize the many advantages this mindset brings.

Growing up without letting my preconceived notions or filters change my perspective has allowed me to approach the world with an open mind, helping me to understand complex issues more clearly before jumping to conclusions. Whether it's engaging in discussions with people from different backgrounds or immersing myself in new cultures, I find that each interaction enriches my understanding of humanity.

While I'm not claiming to be completely unbiased--after all, everyone carries their own set of beliefs and values but, I've learned to adopt a mindset that acknowledges the validity of diverse viewpoints. By reminding myself that just because something doesn't align with my beliefs doesn't mean it's wrong or bad, I've cultivated a sense of curiosity and respect for differences.

It's a continuous practice to strive for openness, to give everything and everyone a fair chance before forming my opinions. This approach not only broadens my horizons but also fosters deeper connections with others, as I learn to appreciate the unique stories and insights they bring to the table. In a world that often feels polarized, I find comfort in the idea that embracing diversity can lead to richer, more meaningful conversations and ultimately, a greater understanding of the human experience.

4

Dream Big

"Dreams should always be a size too big, so you can grow into them"

Unknown

It's no secret that dreams have the power to shape our lives. They ignite our imagination, fuel our passion, and propel us towards the extraordinary. So, never hold back when it comes to dreaming. Let your mind soar to unimaginable heights and embrace the wild and audacious dreams that whisper to your soul.

When we dream big, we tap into a limitless reservoir of possibilities. It's like unlocking a hidden door that leads to a world where everything is within our reach. So why settle for mediocrity when you have the power to dream beyond boundaries? Allow your aspirations to stretch the limits of what you believe is possible because it is in the pursuit of these proud dreams that we truly discover our potential.

The thrill of pursuing something greater than yourself can be intoxicating. It fuels your every step, pushing you forward even when faced with setbacks and challenges. Embrace the uncertainty and the challenges that come with dreaming big because they are the stepping stones that will forge your character and resilience.

Dreaming big requires courage -the courage to believe in yourself, in your abilities, and in your vision for an extraordinary future. It takes courage to ignore those who doubt or belittle your dreams. Remember, it is not the size of the dream itself that matters; it is about having unwavering belief in its possibility and having the determination to see it through.

Dreaming big requires perseverance -the perseverance needed not only to start but also to keep going even when progress seems slow or nonexistent. It's about the ability to stay committed and focused on your dream, even when the road ahead seems long and arduous.

So, don't be afraid to dream with all your might. Dream big and let your imagination run wild. Trust yourself and trust that the universe is conspiring in your favor. Surround yourself with people who support and believe in your dreams. Seek out mentors who have walked similar paths and learn from their experiences.

As you embark on this journey of dreaming big, remember that failure is not a sign of defeat but rather an opportunity for growth. Embrace failures as valuable lessons that will ultimately propel you forward towards success.

Dreaming big requires patience -the patience to understand that dreams take time to materialize. Rome wasn't built in a day, and neither will your dreams come true overnight. Trust the process, stay committed, and celebrate every small milestone along the way.

Never underestimate the power of dreaming big. It has the potential to transform not only your life but also the lives of those around you.

"It always seems impossible until its done"
Nelson Mandela

Dreams have an incredible ability to shape our thoughts, actions, and ultimately, our destinies. We all have dreams - dreams of accomplishing things, and dreams of creating a life that fills our hearts with joy. These dreams are not meant to be idle fantasies but rather powerful catalysts for growth and transformation.

In the pursuit of our dreams, it is paramount that we dream big - unapologetically big. It is in dreaming big that we allow ourselves to tap into the limitless potential within us. No dream should be deemed too audacious or unattainable; instead, we should embrace them fearlessly and let them guide us towards becoming the best version of ourselves.

It is said that our subconscious mind plays a crucial role in manifesting our dreams into reality. This mighty force within us acts as a faithful servant tirelessly working behind the scenes to align our thoughts and actions with what we desire most. When we truly believe in our dreams and hold unwavering faith in their realization, the power of the subconscious mind is unleashed.

Imagine your subconscious mind as a wellspring overflowing with creative energy waiting to be harnessed. Miracles are created through the link between our conscious desires and our subconscious beliefs. The universe conspires with unwavering support when we dare to dream big and set forth on a path towards making those dreams come truc.

But how do we tap into this immense power? How do we bridge the gap between where we are now and where we want to be?

The answer lies in unwavering belief - belief not only in ourselves but also in the universe's ability to bring forth what we envision. It requires cultivating an unshakable faith that everything needed for success will unfold before us at the perfect time.

Dreaming big is not about wishful thinking or idle daydreaming. It's about making progress each day toward achieving the dream you aspire to turn into reality. It's about always keeping your focus on your ultimate goal and never losing sight of it. It is about embracing a mindset of possibility and actively working towards our goals while staying open to unexpected opportunities and synchronicities that may arise along the way.

When we dare to dream big, we set in motion a series of events that align with our desires. Doors open, connections are made, and resources are drawn to us like moths to a flame. It will seem like the universe is working in harmony with us, leading us toward achieving our dreams with each breath we take.

But make no mistake; dreaming big requires courage. It demands that we step outside our comfort zones and face our fears head-on. It asks us to become vulnerable, to challenge societal norms and expectations, and to persist even in the face of adversity.

Dreaming big is not for the faint-hearted but rather for those who are willing to embrace discomfort in pursuit of their passions. It requires discipline, resilience, and an unwavering commitment not only to ourselves but also to the life, we envision for ourselves.

Dreaming big is not just a whimsical notion; there is actual scientific evidence to support the idea that having grand aspirations can lead to numerous benefits and a happier life overall. Studies have shown that individuals who set ambitious goals for themselves tend to experience higher levels of motivation and persistence in pursuing their dreams.

When we dream big, our brains are stimulated to think creatively and problem-solve, leading to increased cognitive flexibility and resilience to challenges. This mindset of aiming high can also boost our self-confidence and belief in our abilities, empowering us to take risks and step out of our comfort zones.

"Shoot for the moon. Even if you miss, you'll land among the stars"
Norman Vincent Peale

Moreover, dreaming big can have a positive impact on our overall well-being and happiness. Research has found that individuals who have big dreams and set challenging goals for themselves tend to experience greater levels of satisfaction and fulfillment in their lives. By striving towards ambitious goals, we not only achieve personal growth and development but also cultivate a sense of purpose and direction.

This sense of purpose can enhance our mental health and emotional well-being, leading to a more positive outlook on life and a greater sense of fulfillment. So, the next time you catch yourself dreaming big, remember that you are not just indulging in fantasy but setting yourself up for a happier and more fulfilling life.

Growing up, I was fortunate enough to have a guiding light of inspiration and unwavering support in my father. His encouragement knew no bounds; he instilled within me an unwavering belief in dreaming big — even bigger than what my logical mind could fathom. Through his constant encouragement and uplifting words, he shattered my

self-imposed limitations and ignited within me an unyielding
spirit.

I've always been someone plagued by self-doubt - someone who
questioned their worthiness at every turn. The world seemed
filled with individuals more accomplished than I could ever
hope to be. But my Dad changed everything; he saw beyond my
insecurities and recognized the redeeming qualities within
me.
With each passing day, he never failed to praise me for even
the smallest achievements - reminding me that progress is
not measured solely by grand milestones but also by small
steps forward. This unwavering support created a safe space
where failure was merely a stepping stone toward growth
rather than an indictment of my capabilities.

"Think big," my dad used to tell me. "There are endless
possibilities out there just waiting for you to grab hold of
them. Why limit yourself to small dreams when you can dream
as big as the sky?"
In those moments, I felt like I could conquer anything -
like there was no challenge too tough to tackle. With my dad
cheering me on, I set off on a journey filled with bold
dreams and unstoppable determination, writing this book is
one of them.
Over the years, I've come to realize that dreaming big isn't
just about wishing for things; it's about recognizing our
potential for growth and change. It's about understanding
that we can push past our limits and create a reality that
goes beyond what we ever imagined.

To accomplish anything, whether large or small, it's essential to have
a guiding principle—something you can consistently pursue. This
principle acts as a compass, directing your efforts and providing clarity
in moments of confusion or uncertainty. It serves as a reminder of why
you started in the first place and helps you maintain your motivation
when faced with challenges.

My dad used to say, "Start and you'll finish it," a phrase that has resonated with me since childhood. His words carry a simplicity that undermines their power, reminding me that the journey toward achieving something significant doesn't always require monumental efforts. Instead, it emphasizes the importance of taking that first step, no matter how daunting the road ahead may seem.

At first, I struggled to grasp the meaning behind his advice. I thought, "Of course you'll finish if you start." It seemed like a simple enough concept, almost too straightforward to be of any real value. However, as I mulled over his words, I began to realize that he was encouraging me to view my goals not just as distant aspirations or items on a to-do list, but rather as a guiding force--or as my dad says a north star. This metaphor resonated with me as it suggested that while my goals should always be present in my thoughts, they shouldn't overshadow the moment or weigh heavily on my mind. Instead of feeling overwhelmed by the sheer magnitude of what I wanted to accomplish, I learned to focus on the path ahead, allowing my ambitions to illuminate my journey without becoming a source of anxiety.

Once I internalized this perspective, it transformed my approach to productivity and personal growth. Suddenly, my cluttered, overstimulated brain felt a little clearer. The constant barrage of tasks and responsibilities that had once felt un completable became manageable as I started to break them down into smaller, more achievable steps. I found myself prioritizing what truly mattered and gave myself permission to celebrate small victories along the way. Each completed task, no matter how insignificant it seemed, became a stepping stone leading me closer to my larger goals. This newfound clarity not only improved my efficiency but also rekindled my motivation, making the journey toward

my aspirations feel more like an exciting adventure rather
than a daunting chore.

As someone who often finds myself caught up in overthinking,
I know firsthand how easy it can be to feel overwhelmed by
the road ahead. The fear of failure or the pressure to
achieve perfection can be paralyzing, making it tempting to
procrastinate or even abandon goals altogether. However, my
father's advice serves as a grounding reminder that the act
of starting is in itself a victory. It encourages me to
shift my focus away from the final outcome and instead
concentrate on the process. Every day, I strive to take even
the smallest step forward--be it jotting down ideas, setting
aside time for practice, or simply reflecting on my
progress. These actions, although they may seem minor in
isolation, are crucial building blocks that pave the way
towards realizing my dreams.

So here's to dreaming big – to reaching for the stars and tapping into
the endless possibilities within each of us. Let's kick self-doubt to the
curb and embrace our dreams with open arms, knowing they have the
power to shape our lives in amazing ways.

As we navigate through life's twists and turns, let's remember that
dreams are meant to be pursued with passion and determination. This
is what living is all about.

Together, let's create a world where dreams aren't just dreams, but
amazing realities."

5

Law of Manifestation

"What you think you become, what you feel you attract, what you imagine you create"
Buddha

Manifestation is the process of realizing your desires and goals into reality through focused intention and steadfast belief. It operates on the premise that the thoughts and feelings you cultivate can influence the outcomes you experience in your life. Essentially, manifestation is about aligning your mindset and actions to attract and achieve what you want.

At its core, manifestation involves the idea that our thoughts and beliefs can shape our reality. The basic principle is that if you can clearly envision your goals and genuinely believe in their possibility, you create a powerful energy that attracts those goals into your life. This concept is often summarized by the phrase "thoughts become things," suggesting that the nature of your thoughts directly impacts the reality you experience.

Intentional thinking is the practice of focusing your thoughts and energy on what you want to achieve. It's not just about wishful thinking but about setting clear intentions and maintaining a positive mindset. When you think intentionally, you direct your mental energy towards your goals, which helps to create a sense of purpose and motivation.

For example, if you want to manifest a new job, you might start by visualizing what that job looks like, how it feels, and what steps you need to take to get there. By focusing on these aspects, you align your actions with your intentions, making it easier to recognize opportunities and take necessary steps toward achieving your goal.

Belief plays a crucial role in manifestation. If you believe that you are capable of achieving your goals and that they are within reach, you are more likely to take proactive steps and remain motivated. On the flip side, if you harbor doubts or negative beliefs about your ability to achieve something, those doubts can hinder your progress.

Expecting positive outcomes also reinforces the power of manifestation. When you expect good things to happen, you are more likely to notice and seize opportunities that align with your goals. This optimistic outlook creates a self-fulfilling prophecy where your positive expectations lead to positive results.

Visualization and affirmations are two powerful techniques used in manifestation. Visualization involves creating a mental image of your desired outcome and immersing yourself in the experience as if it has already happened. For example, if you want to manifest a successful career, you might visualize yourself excelling in your role, feeling satisfied, and receiving recognition.

Affirmations are positive statements that reinforce your goals and beliefs. By repeating affirmations related to your desires, you reinforce a positive mindset and counteract any self-doubt. For instance, affirmations like "I am confident and capable of achieving my goals" can help to shift your mindset towards success.

Manifestation isn't just about thinking positively; it also involves taking action. Aligning your actions with your intentions is crucial for bringing your desires into reality. This means setting practical goals, making informed decisions, and taking consistent steps toward achieving what you want.

Gratitude is a vital component of the manifestation process. By expressing gratitude for what you have and for the progress you make, you create a positive energy that attracts more of what you desire. Gratitude shifts your focus from what's lacking to what's already present, fostering a mindset of abundance and attracting further positive experiences.

Manifestation requires patience and flexibility. While it's important to have a clear vision of your goals, it's also essential to remain open to unexpected opportunities and changes. Sometimes, the path to achieving your goals may take unexpected turns, and being flexible allows you to adapt and embrace new possibilities.

In summary manifestation is a powerful process of turning your desires into reality through focused intention, belief, and aligned action. By cultivating a positive mindset, visualizing your goals, using affirmations, and taking practical steps, you create a powerful force that attracts and manifests your desires. Combining these practices with gratitude, patience, and flexibility enhances the effectiveness of manifestation and helps you achieve a fulfilling and successful life.

Embrace the art of manifestation as a tool for shaping your reality and creating the life you envision. Your thoughts, beliefs, and actions have the power to transform your dreams into tangible achievements.

I stumbled upon the concept of manifestation when I attended a book fair with my dad, where we came across a book titled "The Secret." The title caught my eye, so we decided to purchase it.

At just eight years old, I surprisingly found myself reading it on my own, which was a big deal since I wasn't much of a reader back then. While I was absorbed in the book, my dad took the initiative to look into its background and discovered that it was quite a well-known self-help book. He became fascinated by the techniques it offered and dove headfirst into the realms of manifestation and meditation.

A few days later, we eagerly began to integrate these techniques into our everyday routines. My dad, my grandma, and I would gather in the living room, taking a few moments each day to practice meditation and affirmations together. It became a cherished family ritual, and I could feel the positive energy surrounding us. The act of focusing on our goals and visualizing our dreams transformed how I approached life. I began to see manifestation not just as a mystical concept but as a practical tool that could help me navigate my aspirations.

Over time, I've applied the law of manifestation countless times, achieving everything from simple wishes, like finding a lost toy, to bigger goals, such as excelling in school and pursuing my passions. Each success served as a reminder of the power of intention, solidifying my belief in the process and encouraging my family to continue exploring this enriching journey together.

"The words you speak turn into the house you live in"
    Hafiz

31

6

Be Bold

Have you ever felt like you're living your life according to what society expects of you? It's a common experience, but it's essential to remember that you have the power to make your own choices and live a life that truly makes you happy.

In a world filled with constant comparisons and pressure to conform, it's easy to get caught up in the fear of missing out (FOMO) and feel obligated to do everything your friends or peers are doing. But here's the truth - you don't have to. It's perfectly okay to march to the beat of your own drum and pursue your own interests. In fact, it's often those who dare to be different and follow their true passions who end up making the biggest impact in the world.

So, how do we break free from societal expectations and embrace our unique path? The first step is learning how to say no. Don't let anyone pressure you into doing something that doesn't align with your values or desires. It is challenging, but remember that it's your life, after all! Take ownership of it.

Saying no can be liberating. By refusing to succumb to FOMO, you open yourself up to a world of possibilities aligned with your authentic self. You don't have to do everything just because everyone else is doing it. Instead, take a step back and ask yourself what truly brings you joy and fulfillment.

Embracing your true hobbies and interests can lead you on an extraordinary journey of self-discovery. Maybe you've always had a passion for painting or playing an instrument but never pursued it because others didn't share the same enthusiasm. Well, now is the time! Don't be afraid any more - dive headfirst into what genuinely ignites your soul.

Sometimes, the simple act of doing something on your own can be incredibly liberating. It could be as easy as going to see that movie your friends weren't interested in, and enjoying every moment of it in the theater by yourself. Or perhaps it's cranking up your eccentric playlist on the speaker, just because you feel like it.

These small moments of independence can be surprisingly empowering and refreshing. There is a unique sense of freedom that comes with embracing your own company and doing things on your own terms.

Whether it's indulging in a guilty pleasure movie or blasting your favorite tunes without worrying about others' opinions, these moments allow you to truly be yourself. So, don't be afraid to march to the beat of your own drum and savor the joy and independence that comes with enjoying your own company.

Remember that there is no right or wrong way when it comes to finding happiness in life. Each person's journey is unique, and what works for others may not work for you. That's why it's crucial to listen to your own inner voice and trust your instincts. Be bold enough to make your own rules.

It won't always be easy, though. You may face criticism or feel like an outsider at times but, embrace your uniqueness and let it guide you towards a life that fulfills you. Trust that by staying true to yourself, you'll attract the right people and opportunities into your life - those who appreciate you for who you are.

When we live authentically, we not only find happiness but also inspire others to do the same. Our courage becomes contagious, encouraging those around us to break free from societal expectations and embrace their own unique paths as well.

It's no secret that society can exert immense pressure on individuals to conform to certain expectations. From what we should wear to the career path we should choose, it can be overwhelming to keep up with all the standards set for us. However, living our lives according to someone else's expectations should never be an obligation.

We must always remember that we are the ones who ultimately have to live with the choices we make. So why not make choices that align with our own passions and desires? Whether it's pursuing a career that truly excites us or being with someone who makes us happy regardless of others' opinions, we should always do what feels right for ourselves.

When I say regardless of others opinions i don't mean the opinions of our well wishers or loved ones. If we're lucky enough to have well wishers in our lives, it's wise to pay attention to their insights. They often have a clear perspective on our goals and can guide us toward the best paths to achieve them. We should value their advice as it's usually given with good intentions and can help us make informed choices. However, ultimately, it's important to trust our own instincts and make decisions that feel right for us.

In a world where everyone seems to follow the herd like a sheep, it's time for us to step back and evaluate if the choices we're making are truly what we want.

Living life on our own terms requires courage, resilience, and a deep understanding of ourselves. It means embracing our uniqueness and celebrating our individuality without fear of judgment or rejection. It's all about having the courage to dream big and going after those goals that light a spark inside of us.

As human beings, we often seek validation from others. We want approval and acceptance from society because it gives us a sense of belonging. However, true fulfillment and sense of belonging comes from within ourselves.

Making choices based on what feels right for us is not selfish; it is an act of self-care and self-love. It allows us to create a life that is authentic and meaningful—something worth waking up for every morning.

Living life on our own terms means overcoming the restricting beliefs imposed on us by society or even by our own thoughts. We must question the traditional standards that hinder our progress and have the courage to create our own unique journey. It may mean stepping out of our comfort zones, taking risks, and facing uncertainty, but it is through these experiences that we grow and evolve.

Living life on our own terms is not about rebelling against society or disregarding the opinions of others. It's about reclaiming our power and autonomy, recognizing that we have the right to design our own lives. It's about finding the balance between staying true to ourselves while respecting and valuing the perspectives of those around us.

In this journey towards living life on our own terms, it's crucial to surround ourselves with people who support and encourage us.

As we embark on this path less taken, let's remember that there will be obstacles along the way. We may face criticism or encounter setbacks. However, it is during these moments that we need to reaffirm our commitment to ourselves.

Living life on our own terms does not guarantee a smooth ride or a perfect outcome. But what it guarantees is a life filled with authenticity, fulfillment, and personal growth—a life that we can truly call our own.

So let's dare to be bold—break free from societal expectations—and make choices based on what feels right for us. Remember: You are in control of your own happiness and fulfillment.

"Fortune favors the bold"
Unknown

7

Be Strong

"Never trust your fears they don't know your strength"
Athena Singh

Standing up for yourself can be a daunting task, but it is crucial not to let others push you around. As Elizabeth Olsen wisely said, "No is a full sentence," meaning you do not owe anyone an explanation beyond that. If someone makes you uncomfortable or tries to pressure you into something, it is within your rights to be intimidating and assertive.

"If you don't control your own narrative someone else will"
unknown

Bullying is an issue that many of us have encountered at some point in our lives, myself included. It can be especially challenging during our formative years when we are still discovering our identities and are more susceptible to negative influences. I understand firsthand how difficult this can be.

During my younger years, I often found myself as the "odd one out" in my social circle. I was the target of teasing and name-calling, with remarks about my weight, appearance, family situation, skin color, or personality constantly thrown my way. It seemed like every aspect of who I was became fair game for jokes and criticisms. This continued until I reached around 12 years old.

Over time, however, I began to find my voice and stand up for myself. It was undoubtedly tough at first but gradually i removed myself from disrespectful situations. This journey presented numerous challenges along the way but, looking back now; I am immensely proud of how far I have come.

As a young girl desperately seeking acceptance and friendship above all else, I would often brush off hurtful comments directed towards me in the hopes that those who teased me were truly my friends. However, it took me quite some time to realize that these individuals were not genuine friends at all and that their hurtful words were not mere jokes.
It was through this realization that I embarked on a journey of self-resilience. I learned to stand up for myself and understand that the behavior exhibited by those who bullied me was a reflection of their own insecurities rather than a measure of my worth. It was not an easy path, but one that ultimately led me to reclaim my power.

In our quest for personal growth and empowerment, it is essential to recognize that standing up for oneself does not equate to aggression or retaliation. Instead, it is about asserting our boundaries and refusing to accept mistreatment. By doing so, we send a clear message that we are worthy of respect and will not tolerate being treated as anything less.

Through my experiences, I have come to understand that strength lies within each one of us. It may take time to find it, but once we tap into our inner reservoirs of resilience and determination, there is no limit to what we can achieve.

So remember, Be strong. Stand tall in the face of adversity. Refuse to let others define your worth. Embrace your uniqueness and celebrate the qualities that make you who you are. Above all else, never forget that you have the power within you to overcome any obstacle life throws your way.

"Though times never last but tough people do"
Robert H. Schuller

* * *

Self Confidence

Confidence is a quality that many of us struggle to possess. It can often feel elusive, like a distant dream that we may never achieve. But confidence can be cultivated, even if it doesn't come naturally? Sometimes, all it takes is a little bit of acting - faking it until you make it.

When we project confidence, something magical happens. We start to feel more powerful and in control. The way we carry ourselves changes, and others begin to perceive us differently as well. It's a subtle shift, but one that can have a profound impact on our lives.

But confidence alone is not enough. To truly navigate the world with grace and wisdom, we must also cultivate self-awareness and perceptiveness. By paying attention to how people make us feel, we can start to identify those who drain our energy - the so-called energy vampires.

When I was younger, I struggled with speaking up and expressing my thoughts and opinions. I believed that it was better to remain invisible - an observer rather than an active participant in life's conversations. Looking back now, I realize how toxic that mindset was.

Speaking up is essential for personal growth and fostering healthy relationships. In environments where mutual respect exists, disagreement should be welcomed as an opportunity for growth rather than feared as a threat to harmony.

Learning to speak up was not an easy journey for me; however, I've come a long way since then. I now understand the value of my thoughts and ideas and have the confidence to share them openly with others. This transformation has had a tremendous impact on my life.

If you find yourself struggling to speak up, know that you are not alone. Many others share this struggle, but it's important to remember that it is worth working on. With time and practice, you can learn to be more vocal and confident in expressing yourself.

When we enter a room, we should do so with confidence and boldness. We should not shy away or try to blend into the background. Instead, we should embrace our unique qualities and showcase our talents with pride.

Taking up space does not mean being arrogant or demanding

attention for the sake of it. It means recognizing our worthiness to be seen and heard - acknowledging that our thoughts, opinions, and ideas are valuable contributions to any conversation or situation.

It's time for us all to step into our power unapologetically. Let's no longer hide behind self-doubt or fear of judgment. We are capable of amazing things, and the world deserves the chance to witness us.

By embracing these principles of confidence, self-awareness, and perceptiveness, you will become better equipped to stand up for yourself while also being mindful of the people and energy around you.

8

Be a Thinker and a Tinkerer

Life is a journey filled with twists and turns, ups and downs. In order to navigate this unpredictable path, it is essential to cultivate the mindset of both a thinker and a tinkerer. These two complementary approaches to life can empower us to face challenges head-on, overcome obstacles, and unlock our full potential.

To be a thinker means to exercise our mental faculties, constantly seeking knowledge, analyzing situations, and developing critical thinking skills. Thinkers are individuals who possess the ability to approach problems from different perspectives, challenge assumptions, and come up with innovative solutions. They understand that there is always more than one way to solve a problem or approach a situation.

By adopting the mindset of a thinker, we open ourselves up to endless possibilities. Instead of settling for conventional wisdom or accepting things at face value, we delve deeper into the complexities of life. We question societal norms, challenge existing beliefs, and explore alternative viewpoints. This intellectual curiosity fuels our personal growth as we strive for greater understanding and enlightenment.

However, being a thinker alone is not enough. The mindset of a tinkerer complements that of a thinker by emphasizing the importance of taking action and trying out different approaches. Tinkerers are individuals who are not afraid to experiment, make mistakes along the way, and learn from them. They understand that failure is not an endpoint but rather an opportunity for growth.

Tinkering allows us to adapt quickly in an ever-changing world. It encourages us to step out of our comfort zones and embrace new experiences. By experimenting with different ideas or strategies, we gain valuable insights into what works best for us personally. Each iteration brings us closer to refining our skills or ideas until they reach their full potential.

When we combine the mindset of both a thinker and a tinkerer within ourselves, we become unstoppable forces capable of overcoming any obstacle that comes our way.

Imagine a scenario where you are faced with a daunting challenge. As a thinker, you analyze the situation from various angles, examining the underlying causes and potential solutions. You challenge your assumptions and question the status quo. But being a tinkerer, you don't stop at analysis; you take action.

You begin experimenting with different approaches, even if they seem unconventional or risky. The fear of failure does not hold you back because you understand that mistakes are part of the learning process. You learn from each misstep, adjusting your course until you find the most effective solution.

The combination of thinking and tinkering enables us to continuously grow and improve ourselves. It encourages us to embrace change instead of fearing it. We become adaptable individuals who can thrive in any circumstance, no matter how challenging.

I have always been a crafty individual, able to create something out of whatever resources are available to me. This talent is something I picked up from my dad, who has always been resourceful and creative in his approach to life. One of the key lessons he imparted to me was the importance of making the best of any situation, much like Tinker Bell from Peter Pan. Tinker Bell's ability to transform ordinary objects into useful tools has always been an inspiration to me, reminding me to look for the potential in everything around me and to never underestimate the power of creativity.

Growing up, my dad and I would often work on DIY projects together, using everyday items to create something unique and practical. Whether it was re-purposing old furniture or finding new uses for household objects, my dad taught me the value of thinking outside the box and finding innovative solutions to everyday problems. This mindset has not only helped me develop my creative skills but has also instilled in me a sense of resilience and adaptability. I am grateful for the lessons my dad has imparted to me and for the inspiration I continue to draw from Tinker Bell's mantra of making something useful out of seemingly ordinary things.

So let us embrace this philosophy - to be both thinkers and tinkerers - as we journey through life's ups and downs. Let us constantly seek knowledge, analyze situations critically, experiment fearlessly, and learn from our experiences.

By doing so, we permit ourselves to explore uncharted territories, discover hidden talents within ourselves, and make the most out of every situation that comes our way.

Growing up, Tinkerbell was one of my all-time favorite characters. From her vibrant personality to her remarkable ability to create magic from seemingly nothing, Tinkerbell stood out to me as a symbol of creativity and resilience. I've always admired her ingenuity and the way she makes the most out of whatever she has on hand. Her unwavering positivity and belief that she can tackle any challenge resonate with me deeply. I see a lot of myself in her; I love to repurpose old items and find creative solutions to problems while maintaining an optimistic outlook. Whether it's transforming an old mason jar into a stylish planter or finding new uses for scraps of fabric, I find joy in giving new life to things that might otherwise be discarded. My dad and I both value resourcefulness and have a strong commitment to being environmentally conscious.

I take great pride in my ability to think outside the box and make use of what's around me. It's not just a hobby; it's a way of life that reflects my values. It's important to clarify that being resourceful doesn't mean being cheap; rather, it's about creativity and sustainability--qualities I truly cherish in myself. Embracing a mindset of resourcefulness allows me to approach challenges with an open mind. This idea has shaped not only my personal projects but also my lifestyle choices, as I strive to minimize waste and promote sustainability in my everyday life. Whether I'm fixing something instead of buying new or choosing to upcycle materials for a new project, I feel a sense of fulfillment that I believe aligns with the spirit of Tinkerbell. In a world where consumption often overshadows creativity, I find inspiration in her character, fueling my passion for making a positive impact through resourcefulness and a hopeful outlook.

By embracing this philosophy of being both a thinker and a tinkerer in all aspects of our lives – personal or professional – we can truly master the art of perception.

9

Wealth and Abundance

In our modern society, money is often seen as the ultimate measure of success and happiness. This perception has been shaped by a multitude of factors, including media portrayals of wealth, social status, and the relentless advertisements that bombard us daily. From luxury cars to extravagant vacations, the images we consume create an idealized version of life that suggests financial abundance equates to fulfillment.

Many people find themselves in a constant chase for higher salaries, better job titles, and the latest consumer goods, convinced that accumulating wealth will bring them the contentment and respect they seek. This relentless pursuit can lead to a cycle of stress and dissatisfaction, as individuals often tie their self-worth to their financial status, believing that having more will automatically make them happier.

However, the reality is that money, while necessary for meeting basic needs and providing comfort, does not guarantee happiness or a sense of achievement. Numerous studies have shown that beyond a certain point, increased income has diminishing returns on overall life satisfaction. People often find true fulfillment in relationships, personal growth, and experiences rather than material possessions. The pressure to attain financial success can overshadow the importance of emotional well-being, creativity, and meaningful connections with others. As society continues to grapple with these conflicting notions, it becomes increasingly vital to redefine success in broader terms—emphasizing holistic well-being, community engagement, and personal values over mere financial gain. Ultimately, a more balanced perspective on success can lead to a richer, more fulfilling life that transcends the limitations of monetary wealth.

* * *

Now let's explore the concept of money as a form of energy.

Money, like electricity, water, fire, and wind, operates on the principle that it cannot be created or destroyed; it can only change form. This fundamental truth is essential in grasping the dynamics of wealth. Just as energy flows through various systems, money flows through our lives in a similar manner.

But how do we tap into this flow of wealth? How do we ensure that we are not just hoarding money but actively participating in its circulation?

The answer lies in understanding the art of perception—the ability to see beyond superficial appearances and recognize opportunities where others might overlook them. By sharpening our perception skills, we can identify needs and problems that are yet unmet or unsolved within our communities.

For example, let's consider Sarah—a talented artist with a passion for storytelling through her paintings. She has honed her craft over the years and developed a unique style that captivates viewers' hearts.

Sarah understands that her artwork holds value because it evokes emotions and sparks conversations. She recognizes that her paintings can bring joy, provoke thought, or even heal emotional wounds. Armed with this knowledge, she seeks out individuals or organizations who could benefit from her art.

She approaches local hospitals and offers to donate some of her paintings to their halls and waiting rooms. Sarah understands that these spaces can be sterile and uninspiring for patients and their families. By infusing her artwork into these environments, she not only enhances the aesthetic appeal but also brings comfort and solace to those going through challenging times.

In return for her generosity, Sarah doesn't ask for money but instead requests recognition as the artist behind the paintings. This exposure not only promotes her work but also opens doors to potential clients who appreciate her unique style.

Sarah's story exemplifies the power of perceiving value beyond monetary transactions. By identifying a need within her community—emotional support in hospital settings—she contributes in a way that aligns with her passion while creating opportunities for herself as an artist.

As we move through life in pursuit of riches and success, it's important to understand that true prosperity isn't just about acquiring wealth. It also involves recognizing the power of sharing with others. We should learn to see value in things that others might miss and actively engage in the ongoing flow of wealth and opportunities.

May we all strive to shift our perspective on wealth from one solely focused on accumulation to one rooted in creating positive change through giving and receiving help when needed. By harnessing the flow of money with an open heart and perceptive mind like Sarah did with her artwork donation project at local hospitals, we can unlock a deeper level of fulfillment and contribute to the well-being of our communities.

* * *

As we navigate through the complexities of life, one question often arises: Is it morally acceptable to earn more money than others? This question has provoked much debate and introspection, as our society grapples with issues of income inequality and the pursuit of personal success. In exploring this topic, it is important to consider the intricate interplay between ambition, ethics, and societal impact.

The belief that it is acceptable to earn more money than others finds its roots in the fact that each individual possesses unique skills, experiences, and aspirations. These factors can contribute to varying levels of success and financial gain. The diversity inherent in human abilities means that some individuals may naturally excel in certain areas, leading them to accumulate greater wealth. In such cases, it would seem unjust to restrict their potential for financial growth.

However, while acknowledging these differences in abilities and aspirations, we must also be mindful of the intention behind wanting to earn more. Ambition and hard work are admirable traits that can propel individuals towards financial success. Yet there exists a fine line between healthy ambition and excessive greed. We must tread carefully in our pursuit of wealth and recognize the potential harm our actions may cause.

When considering whether earning more money than others is morally acceptable or not, it becomes imperative to reflect on the impact our actions have on others and society at large. We must ask ourselves if our pursuits are rooted in a desire for personal gain at any cost or if they align with ethical principles that prioritize fairness and well-being for all.

Our society is like a connected network where what we do affects more than just ourselves. When thinking about achieving financial success, it is important to understand and consider how our actions impact others.

An ethical approach requires finding a balance between personal ambitions and ethical behavior. It entails acknowledging the potential consequences of our actions and ensuring they do not come at the expense of exploiting or harming others. It calls for a thoughtful consideration of the well-being of others in our pursuit of financial success.

Striving for personal success need not be synonymous with disregard for moral values. In fact, it is possible to create a harmonious relationship between personal ambitions and ethical conduct. By recognizing that financial success can be achieved while upholding moral principles, we can navigate the complexities of earning more money than others with integrity.

Ultimately, the question of whether it is morally acceptable to earn more money than others cannot be answered definitively. It is subjective and dependent on individual perspectives and values.

However, what remains constant is the importance of self-reflection and critical examination as we navigate these ethical dilemmas.

The art lies in perceiving that financial success does not exist in isolation but rather within a complex web of interconnectedness. It lies in recognizing that personal ambitions can be pursued while simultaneously uplifting others and prioritizing ethical conduct.

In this delicate balance between ambition, ethics, and societal impact lies an opportunity for growth – both individually and collectively. As we strive for financial success, let us aim to embody empathy, integrity, and compassion towards ourselves and those around us.

Greed and ambition

In life, there exists a clear distinction between two forces that drive human actions: greed and ambition. These two powerful motivators can shape destinies, create empires, and even destroy lives. But what sets them apart? And how do they impact the world around us?

Greed, at its core, is a bottomless pit of desire. It is the insatiable hunger for more - more wealth, more power, and more possessions. Greedy individuals are consumed by their own self-interests, always seeking to accumulate and hoard without a thought for others. They view the world as a playground where they can exploit and manipulate to satisfy their insatiable cravings.

"Strive not to be a success, but rather to be of value"
Albert Einstein

Ambition is a powerful force that propels us towards our goals and dreams. It is not merely a desire for success or recognition, but a deep-rooted sense of purpose that drives us to excel and achieve our fullest potential. Unlike greed, which is often driven by a desire for material wealth or power, ambition is fueled by passion and a genuine love for what we do.

When we are driven by ambition, we are driven by a sense of meaning and fulfillment that transcends any external rewards or accolades. It is a drive that comes from within, pushing us to constantly push our limits and strive for excellence. Ambition is not about competing with others or seeking validation from the outside world, but about challenging ourselves to grow and evolve into the best versions of ourselves. So let your ambition guide you, let it inspire you to chase after your dreams with unwavering determination and passion.

Ambitious people celebrate their achievements as milestones on the path towards their dreams. They relish each step forward while never losing sight of the fact that their triumphs are only meaningful when they are shared. These individuals understand that true success is achieved not by stepping on others to climb higher but by lifting others up alongside them.

In the eternal battle between greed and ambition, it is clear which side leads to a more fulfilling and purposeful existence. Greed may provide momentary satisfaction, but it ultimately leaves behind a trail of broken relationships, shattered dreams, and an emptiness that cannot be filled.

Ambition, on the other hand, offers a pathway paved with integrity, collaboration, and genuine fulfillment. Those who embrace ambition as their guiding light find joy in helping others succeed while working tirelessly to achieve their own goals. Their legacy becomes one of inspiration and empowerment rather than selfishness and greed.

As we navigate our own journeys through life's paths, let us remember this crucial distinction between greed and ambition. Let us choose to be driven by purpose rather than insatiable desire; let us strive for success while uplifting those around us.

For it is in this delicate balance between personal achievement and collective growth that we unlock the true art of perception - seeing beyond ourselves to create a world where ambition reigns supreme over greed.

* * *

Money is a complex topic, and while I don't claim to have all the answers, I will do my best to share what I've learned so far. It's important to remember that regardless of how much money you possess or earn, there are limitations on how much you can personally use for yourself and your loved ones. Money is not meant to be hoarded or confined; it is a form of energy that is constantly in motion.

If we think about money as energy, we can draw parallels to other forms of energy in our world. Just like electric energy, water energy, air energy, or fire energy, money has the inherent quality of movement. It flows and spreads out, touching the lives of many in its path. The essence of money lies not in its accumulation but in its ability to impact and improve the lives of others.

In Hindu Scriptures, it is said that Lakshmi - representing wealth or money - is 'chanchanbal' meaning it is unstable. This instability mirrors the nature of energy itself. If we observe various forms of energy around us, we notice their constant movement from one place to another. Understanding this principle allows us to actively facilitate the flow of money. When we open ourselves up to facilitating the movement of money toward positive endeavors we naturally attract more wealth into our own lives. By aligning our intentions with the true purpose of money, we become conduits for this powerful force.

But how do we develop a healthy relationship with our finances? How do we ensure that our actions reflect an understanding and appreciation for the flow and purpose of money? Here are some key considerations:

1. Shift Your Perspective: Instead of viewing money as something solely for personal gain or security, see it as a tool for making a positive impact on the world around you. Understand that its true purpose is to transverse and touch as many lives as it can.

2. Practice Generosity: Cultivate a mindset of giving. Whether it's through charitable donations, supporting local businesses, or helping those in need, strive to share your resources with others. By actively participating in the flow of money, you create a positive cycle that benefits both yourself and those around you.

3. Embrace Abundance: Let go of scarcity thinking and embrace abundance. Recognize that there is more than enough wealth in the world for everyone to thrive. By celebrating the success of others and fostering an abundance mindset, you open yourself up to receiving more financial opportunities.

4. Align Your Actions with Your Values: Ensure that your financial decisions align with your core beliefs and values. Choose consciously where you spend, save, and invest your money, ensuring it supports causes or organizations that reflect what matters most to you.

By nurturing a healthy relationship with our finances - one rooted in purposeful action - we not only invite abundance into our lives but also contribute positively to the world around us. Remember that money is not meant to be hoarded; it is meant to flow freely.

* * *

Flow of Money

Money, in its essence, is not meant to be stagnant. It is more akin to a flowing river than a still pond. Just as water needs to move and flow to remain fresh and pure, money also requires circulation to bring abundance and prosperity. It is through the active engagement in the circulation of wealth that we become conduits for the energy of money.

One way to actively engage in the circulation of wealth is through investments. By wisely investing our resources into ventures that align with our values and goals, we not only have the potential to grow our wealth but also provide support for businesses or initiatives that can benefit others as well.

A practical illustration of this principle is found in the way venture capitalists and angel investors engage with the flow of money. While it might seem like many of the businesses they invest in don't yield strong returns, the few that perform well often make up for the losses and generate significant profits overall.

Another avenue for participating in the flow of abundance is through charitable contributions. When we give selflessly to causes that resonate with us, we create a ripple effect that extends far beyond our own lives. Whether it's donating money or volunteering time and skills, every act contributes to keeping the energy of money in motion.

Supporting small businesses is yet another way to promote financial circulation within communities. By consciously choosing local establishments over larger corporations whenever possible, we help sustain livelihoods while fostering economic growth on a grassroots level.

It's important to recognize that participating in the flow of abundance goes beyond mere financial transactions; it is a mindset and a way of life. It requires us to shift our perspective from scarcity to abundance, from fear to trust. When we view money as a resource meant to be shared and circulated, we open ourselves up to an entirely new level of financial well-being.

As we become active participants in the circulation of wealth, we start experiencing the profound impact it has on our lives. The more we give, the more we receive. The more we contribute, the more opportunities for growth come our way.

By perceiving money as a flowing river rather than a stagnant pond, by actively engaging in its circulation through investments, charitable contributions, and supporting small businesses, we become channels for the flow of abundance. This mindset opens up endless possibilities for financial growth and fulfillment while benefiting not only ourselves but also those around us.

So let us embrace this concept wholeheartedly and watch as the energy of money enriches our lives in ways beyond measure. Together, let's keep the flow going and create a world where prosperity knows no limits.

* * *

I often get asked how I learned about managing money at such a young age. Well, it all started with my dad trusting me with both freedom and responsibilities when it came to finances. Around the age of 14, I was already taking on the role of handling bill payments and grocery shopping in our household. It may sound like a lot for a teenager, but my dad believed in teaching me practical life skills early on.

One of the pivotal moments in my financial education was when my dad handed me my very own debit card at the age of 15. Suddenly, I had a tangible tool in my hands that allowed me to make financial transactions and manage my own expenses. This early introduction to financial independence not only taught me the value of money but also instilled in me a sense of accountability and prudence when it comes to financial decision-making. My dad's guidance and trust in me laid the groundwork for a solid understanding of financial responsibility that has stayed with me into adulthood.

Growing up, my dad was never one to sugarcoat the realities of the world. From a very young age, he made sure that I understood the importance of money and how it influenced our lives. Our conversations about finances were always straightforward and honest, creating a comfortable environment for discussing such topics in our household, topics such as the ones I've mentioned in this chapter were also something my dad taught me, These are ideas he genuinely believes in, he shared these topics after i was a little older so that i could comprehend them.

As a result of open conversations, money was never a taboo subject for me; it was just another aspect of life that I gradually learned to navigate.

Thanks to my dad's open approach to discussing money, I developed a keen awareness of its role in shaping our decisions and actions. Understanding why we made certain choices and how money factored into them became second nature to me. This early exposure to financial matters laid a strong foundation for me to naturally start thinking about budgeting, saving, and planning for the future as I grew older. With my dad's guidance, I effortlessly transitioned into taking on more financial responsibility and learning the value of being mindful and proactive when it comes to managing money.

* * *

Being Humble

In today's society, there is a prevailing culture of flaunting our material possessions. Everywhere we turn, we are bombarded with images and messages that encourage us to showcase our wealth and success. But amidst this frenzy of showmanship, it is crucial to understand the difference between showing off and being humble.

Showing off often involves boasting about our material possessions in a way that can be offensive or provoke envy in others. Some individuals with great wealth revel in flaunting their success, using their possessions as a means to assert their superiority. This act of flaunting is usually accompanied by feelings of pride and self-importance.

It is essential to discover that delicate equilibrium where we can revel in our achievements without wanting to make others feel inadequate or less worthy. Being humble does not mean hiding our success; rather, it means sharing it graciously and with humility.

Humility allows us to appreciate the significance of our accomplishments while recognizing that they do not define us as individuals. It enables us to remain grounded and connected with others on a deeper level. When we find this balance between enjoying what we have earned while remaining respectful towards others' circumstances, we experience profound contentment within ourselves.

Moreover, being humble helps us foster stronger relationships built on mutual respect rather than superficial comparisons based on material possessions. When we approach interactions from a place of modesty instead of arrogance, we create an environment where true connections can flourish. People are more likely to be drawn to us when we exude genuine humility, as it reflects a sense of authenticity and sincerity.

So, the next time you find yourself contemplating showing off your latest acquisition, take a moment to reflect on what your intentions are, are they coming from a place of contentment and humility or from a place of pride and boast? Remember, it is perfectly acceptable to indulge in the fruits of our labor and enjoy the rewards of our hard work. However, it is vital to do so in a manner that does not overshadow the value of humility. Finding that sweet spot between showing off and being humble is an art form worth mastering. It allows us to strike a harmonious balance between enjoying our success and keeping our pride and ego in check.

$$* * *$$

Pride vs Confidence

It's common to get a little confused when it comes to pride and confidence. We often find ourselves teetering on a fine line, not quite sure where one ends and the other begins. In our quest to feel sure of ourselves, we might accidentally slip into the realm of arrogance or dig our heels in too firmly, mistaking it for being determined. So, let's take a moment to dig deeper into these nuances and unravel the mystery of this tricky situation.

Pride, at its core, is rooted in insecurity. It emerges as a defense mechanism against our own perceived inadequacies. When we allow pride to consume us, it becomes an insidious force that pushes us to flaunt our accomplishments and seek validation from others.

Those who cloak themselves in pride often fail to take the time for introspection and self-discovery. They become so entangled in their desire to impress others that they lose touch with their authentic selves. This can lead them down a path of self-destruction.

When someone constantly seeks validation through showing off and prioritizes their own agenda above all else, they become resistant and self-centered individuals. Their need for external approval blinds them from recognizing the impact their actions may have on those around them.

Confidence, on the other hand, stems from a deep understanding of oneself. It is an inner knowing that allows us to trust our abilities without feeling the need to prove ourselves at every turn. Confident individuals exude an aura of self-assuredness that attracts admiration without seeking it.

But how do we distinguish between these two seemingly similar states? The key lies in humility and genuine support towards others. True confidence does not require tearing down others or overshadowing their achievements; instead, it seeks to uplift and inspire.

Confidence is the art of being comfortable in one's own skin, embracing both strengths and weaknesses. It empowers us to take risks, pursue our passions, and stand tall in the face of adversity. It does not rely on external validation but finds its source from within.

As we navigate the intricate dance between pride and confidence, let us strive for authenticity. Let us remember that true strength lies not in overpowering others or showcasing our accomplishments at every opportunity but in embracing our imperfections with grace.

Let's shed the cloak of pride that hinders our true potential and embrace the power of genuine confidence. Let us embark on a path where self-assuredness is rooted in self-awareness, where humility coexists with assertiveness, and where supporting others becomes natural.

Do not be deceived by the allure of pride masquerading as confidence. Seek instead the genuine warmth of self-assurance that comes from understanding oneself deeply. Embrace your strengths with humility and nurture your weaknesses with compassion.

*　*　*

Success

Success, a word that holds different meanings for each individual. It is not something that can be measured by comparing oneself to others but rather a personal journey that must be defined based on one's own values, passions, and goals. To truly understand success, it is crucial to distinguish between achievement and success itself. While achievement revolves around reaching specific goals, success extends beyond mere accomplishments. It encompasses a state of being and a profound feeling of fulfillment.

Success is waking up every morning with an unwavering sense of purpose and a deep understanding of why one pursues their chosen path in life. It involves following one's passion or purpose wholeheartedly, allowing it to guide every decision and action taken. True success lies in living with intentionality and embracing the innate desire to make a meaningful impact in the world.

In contrast, achievements are the tangible markers along the journey towards success. They are the milestones that propel individuals forward, driving them to set new aspirations for themselves once previous goals have been attained. While accomplishments such as wealth, prosperity, or fame may initially bring happiness, these feelings can quickly fade if there is no continuous growth or pursuit of new objectives.

To embark on the path towards true success, one must first define what it means to them individually. Society often imposes its own standards and expectations upon us; however, adhering solely to external measures of success will lead us astray from our authentic selves. A person's version of triumph may differ significantly from another's – for some it may revolve around career advancements or financial stability while for others it could entail nurturing meaningful relationships or making a positive impact on their community.

Embracing our uniqueness allows us to redefine conventional notions of success and carve out paths tailored specifically for ourselves instead of trying to fit into pre-existing molds. It is crucial to align our goals and aspirations with our values, passions, and inner convictions. By doing so, we can authentically pursue a life that brings us joy, fulfillment, and a deep sense of purpose.

As we journey towards success, it is essential to cherish the process rather than solely focusing on the end result. Celebrating every small victory along the way not only keeps our motivation intact but also allows us to appreciate the growth and progress we have made.

Success transcends mere achievements; it is a state of being rooted in purpose and passion. Defining success for oneself enables individuals to break free from external expectations and embark on a unique path tailored specifically to their values and desires. By embracing the process as well as celebrating each milestone along the way, true success becomes an ongoing journey filled with personal growth and fulfillment. So dare to define your own version of success – one that brings you genuine happiness and allows you to make your mark on the world through your unique gifts and talents.

10

Embrace Failure

"It is what you do after failure that defines who you are"
Priyanka Chopra Jonas

"Embrace failure." It was a concept that my father instilled in me during my childhood. He had always encouraged me not to fear failure but to see it as a crucial stepping stone for growth and learning.

In a world where success is often idolized and failures are shunned, it can be easy to forget that even the most accomplished individuals have experienced setbacks. The difference lies in how they choose to respond to these obstacles.

Successful people understand that failure is not an endpoint but a stepping stone towards progress. They refuse to allow their failures to define them; instead, they embrace them as valuable lessons on their path toward greatness.

Life itself is a series of failures waiting to be transformed into triumphs.

From our earliest attempts at walking and talking, we stumble and fall countless times before we find our balance. It is through these initial failures that we learn perseverance and resilience.

But embracing failure goes beyond mere acceptance; it requires a shift in mindset. Rather than viewing failure as something negative or shameful, we should perceive it as an opportunity for growth and self-improvement. Recognize that every misstep brings with it invaluable insights and experiences that can propel us forward.

"Failure is simply an opportunity to begin again more intelligently"
Harrison Ford

One such example is Thomas Edison, the renowned inventor who famously said, "I have not failed 10,000 times—I've successfully found 10,000 ways that will not work." His relentless pursuit of creating the electric light bulb was marked by numerous setbacks and disappointments. Yet he never allowed these failures to deter him from his ultimate goal.

It is this unwavering determination combined with an open-minded approach that enables successful individuals to turn their failures into stepping stones towards success. Each setback becomes an invitation for innovation—a chance to recalibrate their strategies, learn from their mistakes, and ultimately emerge stronger than before.

Embracing failure is not about glorifying mistakes or celebrating setbacks. It is about acknowledging that failure is an integral part of the human experience. By accepting this reality, we free ourselves from the fear of failure and create space for growth and exploration.

But what does it mean to embrace failure? It means reframing our perception of success and adopting a growth mindset. Instead of fixating on the end result, we focus on the process—the journey towards mastery. We understand that success is not linear but rather a series of trial and error.

Embracing failure also involves being willing to step outside our comfort zones and take risks. It requires us to abandon the safety net of familiarity and venture into uncharted territories where failure becomes an inevitable companion. But it is within these moments that we discover our true potential and unlock new possibilities.

So do not be discouraged by failures but see them as stepping-stones on your path towards success. Embrace each setback as an opportunity for growth and learning. Remember that successful individuals are not immune to failures; they simply choose not to let them define their journey.

Failure is a natural part of life, yet accepting it and moving on can be one of the toughest challenges we face. It can feel like a crushing blow to our self-esteem and confidence, leaving us feeling defeated and disheartened. Starting over after a setback requires immense courage and resilience. The fear of failing again can be paralyzing, making it difficult to take that first step forward. The emotional toll of facing failure and having to begin anew can be exhausting and overwhelming. It can be hard to let go of the past and the expectations we had for ourselves, but it is essential in order to move forward and grow.

It is important to remember that failure does not define us. It is simply a temporary setback that presents an opportunity for growth and learning. Embracing failure as a part of the journey towards success can help shift our perspective and enable us to bounce back stronger. It is okay to feel disappointed, frustrated, and even scared, but it is crucial to not let these emotions hold us back. By acknowledging our feelings and allowing ourselves to process them, we can gradually build the resilience needed to overcome failure and start afresh with a renewed sense of determination and purpose.

Remember, it's not about how many times we fall, but how many times we get back up.

In life, setbacks are inevitable. We will all face challenges and obstacles along our journey in life, it is how we choose to respond to these setbacks that truly defines us. Maintaining a positive attitude in the face of failure is crucial if we want to continue moving forward and ultimately achieve our goals.

Successful people often possess a strong positive outlook on life. They understand that life is filled with ups and downs, but they choose to focus on the good and remain hopeful. This unwavering optimism is something I have always admired in my father. Regardless of the circumstances, he has consistently maintained a positive mindset and looks towards a bright future.

Growing up, my father taught me the importance of staying upbeat and positive even when things get tough. He instilled in me the belief that having a positive attitude doesn't mean ignoring the challenges we face; rather, it means staying hopeful and believing in better days ahead, even when things don't go as planned.

This mindset has proven invaluable throughout my own journey. It has helped me overcome countless obstacles, turning failures into opportunities, and keep pushing forward, even when the odds seemed insurmountable.

Our attitude shapes how we perceive the world around us. By consciously choosing to embrace positivity, we can alter our perspective and better react to challenging situations.

Let me reiterate failure does not need to be synonymous with defeat. Embrace failure and let us cultivate a mindset of self-compassion. Instead of berating ourselves for our mistakes or perceived shortcomings, we must learn to treat ourselves with kindness and understanding. This self-compassion allows us to bounce back from failure with renewed determination and a willingness to learn from our mistakes.

Like most people, I've always had a strong aversion to failure. I dreaded being incompetent or not knowing something, feeling that it reflected poorly on me. There was this persistent voice in my head that warned me against even trying; it would whisper, "Why bother? You'll probably fail anyway." This self-doubt often held me back from pursuing new opportunities or pushing myself outside my comfort zone. For a long time, I allowed that fear to dictate my decisions, which created a stifling cycle of hesitation and missed chances. I remember times when I let my insecurities prevent me from speaking up in situations or pursuing projects I was passionate about, all because I was terrified of not meeting expectations or facing judgment.

However, as I've grown older and experienced more of what life has to offer, I've come to understand that you can't experience success without encountering failure along the way. They are two sides of the same coin. Each setback has taught me something invaluable, whether it was a lesson in resilience, humility, or creativity. I've started to see failure not as a reflection of my worth but as an integral part of the learning process. Letting the fear of failure dictate my actions only served to limit my potential and stifle my growth.

Life is far too brief to be paralyzed by the thought of making mistakes. So, I've made a conscious decision to embrace errors as part of my journey, viewing them as stepping stones rather than stumbling blocks. This shift in mindset has not only made me more open to new experiences but has also enriched my understanding of myself and my capabilities.

Embracing failure means re framing our perspective on success. It is not solely measured by the absence of failure but rather by how we respond when faced with it. So the next time you encounter a setback or find yourself facing failure, remember to stay positive, stay hopeful, and keep moving forward because better days lie ahead. Embrace failure as an opportunity for growth and believe in your own ability to overcome any obstacle standing in your way. With the right mindset and unwavering determination, success will be within your reach.

II

Part Two

UNDERSTANDING OTHERS

11

Self Love

"To be beautiful means to be yourself. You don't need to be accepted by others : you need to accept yourself"
Thich Nhat Hanh

Self-love is a journey that extends far beyond the surface-level positivity often associated with it. It is an exploration of one's inner self, encompassing both the light and dark aspects of one's being. It involves embracing all facets of oneself without judgment or condemnation, recognizing that they are integral to our identity. True self-love establishes a firm foundation from which personal growth and improvement can flourish.

In our quest for self-improvement, it is essential to acknowledge and accept ourselves as we are, flaws and imperfections included. By accepting our "flaws" without judgment or shame, we allow them space to be heard and understood. This process allows for healing and growth as we learn valuable lessons from our experiences and transform them into wisdom. Genuine self-love entails loving every part of ourselves unconditionally and wholeheartedly. It does not depend on seeking validation or love from others to fill an internal void. Instead, it requires cultivating a deep sense of self-acceptance and appreciation.

The journey towards self-love begins with understanding that we are inherently worthy of love and respect. We do not need to prove our worthiness or earn the affection of others. Each one of us is born with an intrinsic value that cannot be measured by external standards or the opinions of those around us. From the moment we enter this world, we are deserving of love, kindness, and respect. Embracing this notion can liberate us from the shackles of self-doubt and societal expectations.

However, this realization can be challenging for many of us who have been conditioned by societal norms to seek external validation. We often find ourselves comparing our lives, appearances, achievements, and relationships to those around us in an attempt to measure our worthiness.

To cultivate genuine self-love, we must unlearn these conditioned patterns of thought and behavior. We must recognize that external validation is fleeting; true fulfillment comes from within.

Self-love is more of a journey than a destination, and it's something we have to keep working on every day. It's all about being gentle with ourselves, practicing forgiveness, and having a little patience. Think of it as treating ourselves with the same warmth and understanding that we would show to a close friend. Remember, you deserve that love too.

One powerful tool in cultivating self-love is the practice of self-care. This encompasses activities that nourish our physical, mental, emotional, and spiritual well-being. Engaging in activities that bring us joy, rest, restoration, and fulfillment replenishes our inner reserves of love for ourselves.

Additionally, nurturing healthy boundaries is crucial in fostering self-love. Setting clear limits on how others can treat us and what behaviors we find acceptable ensures that our own needs are respected. Boundaries protect our energy and preserve our sense of self-worth.

* * *

Loving yourself and liking yourself are both essential components of a healthy self-image, yet they encompass different aspects of self-acceptance. Love and like, while often used interchangeably in everyday conversation, have unique implications when it comes to how we perceive ourselves.

To love yourself means to embrace your entire being, accepting both your strengths and weaknesses, and recognizing your intrinsic worth as a person. This deep-rooted affection is about acknowledging your value, nurturing your spirit, and being kind to yourself through life's ups and downs. It's about cultivating a sense of self-compassion that allows you to forgive yourself for past mistakes and to celebrate your achievements, no matter how small they may seem.

On the other hand, liking yourself often relates to the more surface-level aspects of your personality and choices. It involves appreciating who you are in the present moment, enjoying your quirks, and acknowledging the qualities that make you unique. When you like yourself, you engage in self-reflection that helps you identify the things you genuinely enjoy about your character and skills. This can foster a sense of confidence and positivity that enhances your overall well-being.

By nurturing both love and like for yourself, you create a balanced and supportive foundation for personal growth, making it easier to navigate challenges and build healthier relationships with others. In essence, both loving and liking yourself are vital for a fulfilled life, helping you to thrive with authenticity and joy.

I would argue that liking yourself is actually more important than loving yourself, and I speak from personal experience when I say this. When I first began the journey of self-acceptance, I focused on the smaller, more manageable goal of simply liking myself. This shift in perspective was transformative. I noticed that as I started to appreciate my own quirks, strengths, and even my flaws, I became happier and more confident. It was as if a weight had been lifted; I no longer felt the need to seek validation from others. Instead, I found joy in my own company and realized that I genuinely wanted to be friends with the person I saw in the mirror. As I treated myself with the same kindness and respect that I would offer to a close friend, a beautiful transformation took place. I began to engage in activities that brought me joy, set healthy boundaries, and practiced self-compassion.

Over time, this nurturing approach helped me evolve from simply liking myself to genuinely loving who I am. The journey wasn't always easy, but embracing the idea of self-liking laid the foundation for a deeper self-love. I came to understand that by fostering a friendship with myself, I could cultivate a profound sense of happiness and acceptance that would ultimately enrich my relationships with others as well. It's a powerful reminder that self-acceptance is not just about love; it's about appreciation and friendship with oneself that can lead to a fulfilling and joyful life.

* * *

It may sound like a cliché, but the truth is that if we cannot love ourselves, how can we expect others to love us?

I've heard many people argue that they need external validation to feel loved and worthy. They believe that compliments or praise from others are necessary to prove their value and increase their self-confidence. However, relying heavily on external validation for self-confidence can be a dangerous path to follow. Compliments and praise are fleeting and superficial; they can be taken away or influenced by outside circumstances.

Lasting self-love starts from the inside; it doesn't rely on how others see or judge you. It's all about acknowledging your own unique worth and embracing the fact that you are valuable for being you. Self-love is not selfish; it is an essential foundation for building healthier relationships with others. So, instead of seeking love outside ourselves, let us embark on a journey of self-love and make a commitment to love ourselves unconditionally.

To cultivate self-love, start by practicing self-care regularly. Take time out each day for activities that bring you joy and nourish your soul—whether it's reading a book, going for a walk in nature, or indulging in hobbies that make you happy.

Additionally, practice positive affirmations daily. Affirmations are powerful tools that help rewire our subconscious mind with positive beliefs about ourselves. Repeat statements such as, "I am worthy of love," "I am deserving of happiness," and "I love and accept myself unconditionally." Over time, these affirmations will become ingrained in your belief system, boosting your self-esteem and self-worth.

Furthermore, self-reflection is a vital component of self-love. Take the time to examine your thoughts and beliefs about yourself. Are there any negative patterns or limiting beliefs that hold you back from embracing self-love fully? Identify these thought patterns and work on replacing them with positive, empowering ones.

Surround yourself with supportive individuals who uplift and encourage you. Choose friends who celebrate your successes, cheer you on during difficult times, and genuinely care about your well-being. Avoid toxic relationships that drain your energy or undermine your sense of self-worth.

If you find yourself without a support network, it's important to become your own source of strength. Embrace self-love and learn to enjoy your own company. Ultimately, at the end of the day, the only person you can truly rely on is yourself.

Always remember that self-love is an ongoing journey; it's essential to acknowledge that not every day will feel uplifting or empowering. There will be days that seem overwhelmingly heavy, where self-doubt creeps in and we find ourselves spiraling into negative thoughts.

On these days, we might feel like we're at our lowest point, grappling with feelings of inadequacy and frustration. It is perfectly normal to experience this emotional turbulence; after all, we are human, and our mental health can fluctuate just like the weather. It's during these challenging periods that we must remind ourselves that it is okay to feel this way. Recognizing and validating our emotions is the first step towards healing.

Despite these moments of darkness, it's crucial to cultivate a sense of compassion for ourselves. Instead of allowing self-hatred to take the reins, we should strive to be our own allies, offering kindness and support as we would to a friend in need. This could mean allowing ourselves to rest when we feel drained, or perhaps engaging in activities that bring us comfort and joy, no matter how small. Practicing self-love during tough times can be as simple as acknowledging our feelings, writing them down, or reaching out to someone we trust. Ultimately, the journey of self-love is not a straight path; it is filled with bumps and detours that can lead to profound growth. By embracing both our strengths and vulnerabilities, we pave the way for a more authentic and resilient self.

As we continue to cultivate self-love within ourselves, we radiate a sense of confidence that draws others towards us authentically. We attract healthier relationships built on mutual respect and genuine connection.

```
Loving ourselves can feel like a monumental challenge, one I
grapple with regularly. Confronting the truth about
ourselves isn't easy, and acceptance can be even harder.
However, I've come to understand that establishing a solid
base of self-care and kindness is crucial. Without this
foundation, everything we strive to achieve can feel
precarious, like constructing a house over an empty cavern
that could cave in at any moment. To truly become the best
version of ourselves, we need to understand who we are and
where we stand in life. It's essential to dig deep, question
our beliefs, and embrace our identities to find lasting
happiness.
```

* * *

When I was younger, the struggle with self-worth and self-acceptance consumed me. As a teenager, around the age of 13, it felt like I was constantly bombarded with messages that reinforced the notion that I didn't fit the mold of what society deemed beautiful or acceptable.

Being a South Asian girl made it even more challenging, as media and pop culture rarely reflected people who looked like me as beautiful and talented.

Instead, what I saw were representations of beauty that starkly contrasted my features. Girls who resembled me were often relegated to stereotypical comedic roles or as the ugly friend, rather than being portrayed as main characters worthy of admiration and respect. It took me years to unravel these negative beliefs about myself, but through affirmations and practicing self-acceptance, I gradually began to shift my mindset.

I made a conscious decision to stop comparing myself to others and trying to change who I was in order to conform to an idealized image. Instead, I started embracing and loving myself for exactly who I am and how I looked. This transformation didn't happen overnight although I wish it did; it required patience and persistence. But with time, I grew more confident and comfortable in my own skin.

Growing up, I often felt like an outsider, not just in the digital landscape but also in the real world. The absence of representation online only compounded my sense of alienation. I would scroll through social media platforms, hoping to see someone who looked like me or shared similar experiences, but instead, I was met with images and narratives that often excluded people of my background. This lack of visibility made me question my own worth and identity. It felt as though I was invisible, lost in a sea of voices and faces that did not reflect my own. The yearning for connection and validation was a constant presence in my life, intensifying the feelings of inadequacy and self-doubt that were already festering within me.

In addition to the digital void, my real-life experiences

only deepened my struggle with self-love. I was frequently
singled out because of my looks and my race, whether it was
at school, in social settings, or even within my own
community. Remarks that highlighted my differences often
came disguised as jokes or casual comments, but they stung
nonetheless.

All I heard was a barrage of messages telling me that I
didn't belong, that I wasn't good enough as I was. These
experiences made it incredibly challenging to cultivate a
sense of self-acceptance. Instead of embracing my
uniqueness, I found myself shrinking in the face of
criticism, desperately wishing to blend in with the crowd.
It was a long and painful journey to unravel those ingrained
beliefs and begin to appreciate the beauty in my
individuality, but I knew I had to try for my own sake.

If you find yourself grappling with similar issues related to self-love
and acceptance, know that you are not alone on this journey. Take
your time; be compassionate towards yourself along the way. Remind
yourself daily that you are deserving of love and acceptance just as you
are – no changes necessary.

Embrace your true self wholeheartedly because you are truly amazing
just the way you are!

As I reflect on my personal path towards self-love, I realize that it has
been a process of unlearning societal expectations and embracing my
authentic self. It involves acknowledging and celebrating my strengths,
while also accepting my flaws with kindness and compassion.

There are days when self-doubt creeps in, when negative thoughts try
to undermine the progress I have made. In those moments, I remind
myself to be gentle – to treat myself as I would treat a dear friend. I

extend empathy towards myself, offering words of encouragement and reminding myself of all the reasons why I am worthy of love and acceptance.

I have learned that self-love is not about arrogance or selfishness; rather, it is about cultivating a deep sense of respect for ourselves – body, mind, and soul. It involves setting healthy boundaries in relationships, prioritizing self-care without guilt or hesitation, and nurturing our passions and dreams.

Together, let us embark on this path towards self-love – a path that leads us to embrace our true selves unapologetically. Let us cast aside society's narrow definitions of beauty and forge ahead with confidence in our own worthiness.

You are beautiful just as you are – never forget that!
K.K

12

Live Freely

"To live is the rarest thing in the world, most people just exist"
  Oscar Wilde

In a world that often tries to confine us within societal expectations, the art of living freely becomes an essential practice. It is through this practice that we can break free from the shackles of conformity and embrace our authentic selves. Living freely is about making choices that align with who we truly are, allowing us to experience life's richness and beauty in its fullest form.

To live freely means to pursue a career that not only provides financial stability but also fills our souls with fulfillment and purpose. It requires us to be courageous enough to chase after our dreams, even if they seem unconventional or risky. Whether it's becoming an artist, a writer, or starting a business based on our passions, living freely encourages us to step outside the boundaries society has set for us.

But living freely is not just about career choices; it encompasses every aspect of our lives, living freely means giving ourselves permission to indulge in activities that bring us joy and nourish our souls. It encourages us to spend time doing the things we love without guilt or judgment.

However, embracing a life of freedom also requires shedding societal expectations and unapologetically being true to ourselves. We must have the courage to follow our passions, hobbies, and interests without fear of judgment or criticism from others who cannot comprehend the significance of our passions and interests in our lives.

Living freely demands that we surround ourselves with individuals who support and uplift us rather than drag us down with negativity or toxic relationships. These connections act as pillars of strength during times when doubt creeps in, and they serve as a reminder that we are not alone on this journey.

Moreover, living freely often involves a deep sense of responsibility. Freedom is not just about doing whatever one pleases; it's also about respecting others' rights to their own freedoms. It's about finding a balance where your actions enrich your life and the lives of those around you.

When we live freely, we break through the barriers that confine our authenticity. We no longer censor our thoughts or suppress our desires to fit into molds created by others. Instead, we express ourselves boldly and unapologetically. We find the courage to speak our minds, knowing that our opinions matter and have the power to create change in the world.

In this state of freedom, limitations cease to exist. We become unstoppable forces pursuing our dreams and aspirations without holding back. The boundaries that once restricted us crumble away as we embrace the limitless possibilities life has to offer.

Living freely is not always an easy path; it requires dedication and perseverance. It demands that we confront our fears head-on and push past them with unwavering determination. It's about embracing uncertainty and understanding that freedom doesn't always come with guarantees.

There's a beauty in making choices that align with your true self, even if it means facing challenges or stepping out of your comfort zone.
    So let us break free from the constraints that society has placed upon us. Let us embrace a life of freedom and authenticity—a life where every choice aligns with who we truly are at our core.

```
I've always been someone who struggles with
embarrassment--who really enjoys feeling that way, right?
For as long as I can remember, self-consciousness has been a
constant companion, often creeping into my thoughts at the
most inopportune moments. I would overthink interactions,
replaying conversations in my head and worrying about how
others perceived me. Each little misstep felt like a
monumental failure, and I was terrified that people might
see me in an unflattering light. My dad, however, had a
completely different outlook on life. He often said, "It's
only embarrassing if you let it be," a phrase that resonated
deeply with me. I admired that quality in him; it was a kind
of boldness I wished I could embody myself. He seemed so
effortlessly comfortable in his own skin, and I often found
myself wishing I could adopt that same carefree attitude.

Over time, through persistent effort and a lot of
self-reflection, I've managed to shift my mindset. It's been
```

a journey, one filled with ups and downs, but I've gradually learned to let go of those inhibiting thoughts that once held me back. Embracing who I truly am has led to a remarkable difference in my life; I can't imagine going back to my old ways. I've started to view situations through a different lens, recognizing that most people are more focused on their own lives than on critiquing mine. I'm genuinely grateful for the progress I've made thus far. It feels so refreshing to be comfortable in my own skin and to accept my personality, quirks and all, even if I'm not entirely there yet. I have faith that soon enough, I will be fully confident in myself, and the thought of that future excites me.

At the end of the day, if someone is judging me or is thinking that I'm embarrassing, that's their issue, not mine. Their opinions don't define who I am. It's all too easy for people to project their insecurities and biases onto others, often without truly knowing the full story or understanding the complexities of someone's life. When faced with judgment, I try to remind myself that everyone has their own perspective shaped by their experiences, beliefs, and values. While it can sting to feel scrutinized or misunderstood, I refuse to let that negativity seep into my self-worth. I understand that I am a multifaceted individual with my own dreams, struggles, and triumphs, and I won't allow anyone else's limited viewpoint to diminish my sense of self.

Moreover, embracing this mindset has been liberating. I've learned that the energy I invest in worrying about what others think of me could be better spent on self-improvement and pursuing my passions. It's important to cultivate a sense of inner confidence and resilience that comes from knowing my own strengths and values. This doesn't mean I disregard constructive feedback; instead, I choose to filter out the noise of judgment that lacks substance. At the end

of the day, I am in control of my own narrative, and I
choose to surround myself with positivity and support rather
than allow external opinions to dictate my happiness or
self-identity.

In practical terms, living freely might mean different things to different people. For some, it could involve a minimalist lifestyle, where freedom comes from simplicity and detachment from material possessions. For others, it might be about financial independence, where freedom comes from having the means to make choices without being tethered by economic constraints. For many, it involves cultivating relationships and communities that support and celebrate their individuality.

Remember living freely is an art form—an art form that grants us permission to be ourselves wholly and unapologetically. It encourages exploration, embraces diversity, nurtures passions, cultivates support-ive relationships, empowers self-expression, defies limitations, and ultimately leads us towards a life filled with happiness and fulfillment.

Love Freely

Love does not adhere to a predetermined plan; it simply happens when we encounter someone who ignites a fire within us. It has no regard for gender or sexual orientation; it can blossom between any two souls who find solace and connection in one another's presence.

Society may attempt to impose its limitations and stereotypes upon our understanding of love, but we must rise above such restrictions. Love knows no boundaries; it defies categorization and cannot be confined by societal expectations. We must liberate ourselves from the shackles of prejudice and embrace love in all its forms.

To love freely means to rise above societal constraints and embrace love in all its forms. It is about letting go of preconceived notions and accepting love as a natural and nonrestrictive force. For example, a child's love for their pet is unconditional and pure, free from the constraints of societal expectations. In a similar way, the connection between two friends who have a silent understanding and provide each other with profound support demonstrates how love can go beyond the traditional idea of love.

Loving freely does not imply a lack of discernment or wisdom. Instead, it calls for an open heart coupled with thoughtful consideration. Intelligent love acknowledges that to love someone is not to overlook their flaws but to embrace them wholly—imperfections included.

Consider a romantic relationship where partners support each other through personal growth. Intelligent love involves recognizing and celebrating each other's strengths while understanding and accepting each other's shortcomings. It means seeing beyond surface-level attributes and engaging with each other's deeper selves. This type of love requires empathy, active listening, and open communication, turning conflicts into opportunities for growth rather than battlegrounds for power struggles.

For instance, in a partnership where one partner is pursuing a demanding career, intelligent love involves understanding the pressures they face and providing emotional support. It also means celebrating their achievements and milestones, fostering a relationship where both partners feel valued and supported.

In the realm of love, trust is a cornerstone that sustains relationships through life's inevitable challenges. Trust is built on a foundation of consistent support, open communication, and mutual respect. It allows individuals to be vulnerable, secure in the knowledge that their love is steadfast.

Time, both an ally and adversary, tests the depth and resilience of our affections. Intelligent love evolves with the passage of time, adapting to life's changes while keeping the relationship vibrant and alive.

Love is not a solitary endeavor but a shared journey of mutual growth. It encourages both parties to support each other's dreams and aspirations while creating a shared vision of happiness and fulfillment. This collaborative approach to love fosters a sense of partnership where both individuals are inspired to grow and evolve.

In a loving relationship, each person becomes a source of inspiration and motivation. They encourage one another to step out of their comfort zones, explore new possibilities, and unlock their full potential.

Too often, love is approached as if it were a transaction—an exchange of affection, attention, or favors with the expectation of receiving something in return. This transactional mindset limits love's potential, reducing it to a mere arrangement rather than an experience of deep, unconditional connection.

Consider a relationship where one person constantly keeps score of the favors or gestures received versus those given. This approach turns love into a ledger of debits and credits, stripping it of its genuine warmth and spontaneity. True love, however, is not about tallying contributions or expecting reciprocity. It is about giving freely and wholeheartedly, without the anticipation of a return.

For example, think of a parent's love for their child which in its true form is not transactional. A parent might sacrifice sleep, personal time, or even career opportunities for the sake of their child's well-being. This love is not given with the expectation of receiving anything back; it is a pure and selfless form of love that flourishes in its own right. This type of love, unburdened by expectations, demonstrates the essence of giving without the need for reciprocation.

Love manifests in many forms, each valid and valuable in its own right. Whether it's the bond between friends, siblings, cousins, or the nurturing connection between a mentor and a protégé, or the deep emotional and physical intimacy between romantic partners, all forms of love are correct and deserving of recognition. Each form of love enriches our lives in unique ways and contributes to our overall sense of fulfillment.

Consider a long-term friendship where two individuals support each other through life's ups and downs. This friendship may not involve romantic elements, but it provides a deep, sustaining connection. The love between friends is as genuine and important as any other form of love. It is characterized by mutual respect, understanding, and a shared history of experiences.

Similarly, the love between a mentor and a mentee can be profoundly transformative. The mentor offers guidance, wisdom, and support, while the mentee grows and evolves under this nurturing influence. This relationship is not transactional but based on the mutual growth and development of both individuals. It illustrates how love can take on different roles and still be deeply meaningful and impactful.

To love freely is to embrace the boundless nature of this beautiful force within your heart. It means letting go of fear and hesitation, allowing love to flow unrestricted by judgment or prejudice. When we love without constraints, we unlock the true potential of our relationships, deepening connections and creating enduring bonds capable of withstanding life's trials.

Love is a complex and exquisite emotion with the power to transform our lives. It requires us to see beyond surface-level attributes, accepting each other's flaws while celebrating each other's strengths. Love thrives on open communication, honesty, and compassion, catalyzing personal growth and supporting each other's aspirations.

In every form of love, whether it's a romantic partnership, a friendship, or a family bond, the core principle remains the same: to give freely and wholeheartedly. When we let go of expectations and embrace love in all its forms, we experience its true power and beauty. Love, in its purest sense, is a gift—one that, when given without reservation, enriches our lives and the lives of those we cherish.

Unconditional Love

> "If it is conditional it is not love"
> Sadhguru

Unconditional love is the purest form of connection. At its core, love should exist without conditions or limitations. It is not about what is given or received but about a fundamental acceptance of another's essence.

Unconditional love does not depend on actions or circumstances; it remains constant regardless of change. This form of love transcends expectations and judgments. It is about embracing others fully and genuinely, without reservations.

To perceive love in its original form, recognize that it is an unwavering presence. It is the acceptance of flaws and the celebration of authenticity. Love should be a steady foundation, not a fluctuating measure. In its truest state, unconditional love is a reflection of the highest human potential, a bond that remains steadfast and pure, regardless of the external factors.

In practice, this means loving without ulterior motives, offering support without strings attached, and embracing others as they are, not as we wish them to be. This form of love is both an ideal and a reality that we should strive to embody in all our relationships.

Unconditional love also involves patience and resilience. It withstands misunderstandings and conflicts, understanding that imperfections are part of the human experience. It is not about ignoring faults but about loving through them, knowing that each person is a work in progress, deserving of support and respect.

Ultimately, unconditional love is a choice we make each day—a commitment to seeing and valuing the true essence of others. It is a practice of kindness and understanding, one that enriches our relationships and elevates our shared human experience. In embodying this form of love, we not only enhance our connections but also contribute to a more compassionate and unified world.

Whenever I take a moment to reflect on the profound concept of unconditional love, my thoughts inevitably gravitate towards my wonderful grandmother.

She is the living embodiment of selfless love, radiating it in its purest form. It is through her countless actions, big and small, that I have come to understand what unconditional love truly means. From the way she greets me with open arms and a warm smile to the countless sacrifices she has made for our family, her devotion is evident in every gesture. Witnessing the depth of her generosity--given freely and without any strings attached--has always left me in awe. She has no hidden agendas, no rigid expectations, and she embraces me wholeheartedly, loving me for who I am, flaws and all. This unwavering acceptance and encouragement have created a safe space where I can be myself without fear of judgment.

I believe there is so much wisdom to be gained from her example, and I strive to embody the same kind of love in my own life every day. Each time I think of her, I am reminded of the importance of giving love freely and nurturing those around us with kindness and compassion. The lessons she imparts go beyond mere words; they are woven into the fabric of my life and our shared experiences.

I feel incredibly fortunate to have someone as remarkable as her in my life, someone whose love has shaped me in countless ways. Every moment spent with her is a reminder of the beauty of unconditional love, and I am truly grateful for her unwavering support and devotion.

Thank you, Nanamma, for being my guiding light and for teaching me the true essence of love.

13

Emotional Vulnerability

" Being vulnerable is the only way to allow your heart to feel
true pleasure"
  Bob Marley

Emotional vulnerability is a struggle that many individuals face. It can be a daunting task to open up and express our emotions to others, especially when society has conditioned us to believe that showing vulnerability is a sign of weakness. However, it is crucial to understand that vulnerability is not weakness; it is, in fact, a strength. It takes immense courage to allow ourselves to be seen by others without any walls or defense mechanisms. By embracing vulnerability, we can forge deeper connections and relationships with those around us. It is through our willingness to be vulnerable that we gain an understanding and empathy for others.

As I reflect upon this subject matter, one quote resonates deeply within me: "The only way out is through." This powerful statement serves as a reminder that in order for us to grow and move forward, we must confront our problems head-on. It may be tempting to avoid difficult situations or suppress challenging emotions; however, doing so only prolongs the healing process. By acknowledging and addressing our emotions and problems directly, we empower ourselves to overcome them and emerge as stronger individuals.

Moreover, embracing emotional vulnerability allows us the space necessary for processing and working through our own emotions effectively. When we suppress our emotions or push them away, we invite negative consequences into our lives such as increased stress levels, heightened anxiety, and even physical health issues. Therefore, it becomes imperative for us not only to recognize the significance of emotional vulnerability but also actively work towards embracing it in every aspect of our daily lives.

Rather than pushing away or denying our emotions out-right when they arise within us, we should instead choose to sit with them and seek understanding. This conscious decision prevents overwhelming emotional states from dictating impulsive actions on our part. By taking the time needed for genuine self-reflection and emotional processing in these moments of vulnerability, we gain invaluable insights about ourselves while simultaneously fostering greater self-awareness.

It is important to note that emotional vulnerability is not an easy skill to develop. It requires practice, patience, and self-compassion. We must learn to let go of the fear of judgment or rejection that often accompanies the act of being vulnerable. Instead, we should focus on the potential rewards—deeper connections with others, personal growth, and a heightened sense of authenticity.

To cultivate emotional vulnerability within ourselves, we can start by creating a safe space where we feel comfortable expressing our innermost thoughts and feelings. This may involve confiding in a trusted friend or seeking professional guidance through therapy or counseling or it might be as simple as journaling. It is essential that we surround ourselves with individuals who support and validate our emotions rather than dismiss them.

Additionally, practicing self-care techniques such as journaling or engaging in creative outlets can help us explore and process our emotions more effectively. By giving ourselves permission to feel without judgment or shame, we open up pathways for healing and personal growth.

Emotional vulnerability is not a weakness but rather a strength that allows us to forge deeper connections with others while also aiding in our own personal growth and well-being. By embracing vulnerability instead of avoiding it, we provide ourselves with an opportunity for genuine self-reflection and understanding. Let us remember that "The only way out is through," as by facing our emotions head-on and acknowledging their presence within us, we empower ourselves to overcome them and emerge stronger than before.

My dad always stressed the importance of being emotionally open. He believed it was one of life's fundamental truths, a cornerstone that supports our relationships and personal growth. He would often say that true strength lies not in hiding our feelings but in embracing them, no matter how uncomfortable they might be. Vulnerability, in his view, played a vital role in every facet of our existence. He would elaborate on how opening up not only fosters deeper connections with others but also leads to a better understanding of ourselves. During our conversations, he often emphasized the necessity of being honest--not just with others, but with ourselves as well. He believed that being truthful about our feelings and experiences is the first step toward emotional freedom and healing.

In our household, he frequently talked about three core values that shape a person's character: honesty, vulnerability, and dependability. These weren't just abstract concepts for my dad; they were guiding principles that he lived by and expected from those around him. Whether we were having dinner, watching a movie, or taking a walk in the park, he would find a way to weave these values into our conversations. I can still hear him having me repeat those words, almost like a mantra, until they became ingrained in my psyche.
Because of him, these principles are deeply rooted in me, shaping my interactions and decisions every day. Honesty has taught me the importance of transparency in my relationships, allowing me to build trust with friends and family alike. Vulnerability has opened the door to deeper connections, reminding me that sharing my true self can lead to more meaningful interactions. Lastly, dependability has instilled in me a sense of responsibility; I strive to be someone others can count on, which has ultimately strengthened my bonds with those around me.

In a world that often promotes self-reliance and stoicism, I find comfort in the lessons my dad imparted. They guide my actions and choices, shaping not just who I am but also how I interact with the world. His teachings remind me that true strength lies in our ability to be open and authentic, paving the way for genuine connections and a fulfilling life.

So let us strive towards embracing emotional vulnerability in every aspect of our lives; for it is through this openness that true connection and personal transformation flourish.

* * *

In a society that often imposes restrictions on the expression of emotions. We should not suppress our emotions or feel ashamed for showing them. Growing up in a single-parent household, I always felt the need to be strong and independent. I believed that I needed to be tough and handle everything on my own.

This mindset carried over into my teens, and I found myself struggling with emotional vulnerability. I would often shut down my feelings and bottle them up, afraid of being seen as weak or vulnerable. It wasn't until I started experiencing anxiety that I realized that I needed to work on being more emotionally open.

At first, embracing emotional vulnerability was difficult for me. It felt like breaking a rule by allowing myself to feel and express my emotions. However, as I started to open up to others and allow myself to be vulnerable, I began to feel a sense of relief. It was a weight lifted off my shoulders to be able to talk about my feelings and not feel like I had to keep them hidden.

Sometimes it feels like the easiest thing to do is to bottle everything up and hope it goes away on its own. But in reality, nothing good ever comes from that approach. Eventually, those emotions will find a way to come out - whether it's through tears or in a fit of rage.

It's crucially important for us all - men and women alike -to remember that it's okay to feel our feelings. We shouldn't be afraid of letting it all out; whether we choose trusted friends or even just ourselves as listeners doesn't matter as much as acknowledging our emotions' validity.

* * *

In my journey towards emotional openness, I have discovered the power of vulnerability firsthand. By letting go of my fear of being judged or rejected for showing my true emotions, I have found support and understanding from those around me.

While embracing emotional vulnerability is an ongoing process for me - as it is for many - I am proud of myself for pushing past my initial resistance and working towards greater emotional openness. It has allowed me to forge deeper connections with others and find greater peace within myself.

So next time you feel like holding back your emotions, remember that it's better to let them out than keep them in. Embrace your emotional vulnerability as a source of strength rather than weakness. And together, let us create a world where expressing our true feelings is not only accepted but celebrated as an essential part of being human.

* * *

Throughout history, society has perpetuated the misguided belief that men should be stoic and unemotional, associating vulnerability with weakness. However, this perception couldn't be further from the truth. Emotions are an integral part of our human experience, regardless of gender. As the next generation, it is crucial for us to challenge these outdated beliefs and teach the men in our lives that it is not only okay but also healthy to be in touch with their emotions.

By creating a safe space for emotional expression, we can dismantle the harmful stereotypes that perpetuate toxic masculinity. It is vital for us to demonstrate through our actions and words that showing vulnerability does not diminish one's strength or masculinity but rather showcases a depth of character and empathy. We must become allies, encouraging men to share their emotions without judgment or ridicule.

In doing so, we can create a supportive environment where everyone feels comfortable expressing their feelings, regardless of gender. Men have long been burdened by harmful stereotypes that discourage them from embracing their emotions fully. It is time for us to become catalysts for change by teaching and demonstrating how crucial it is to honor and express our emotions.

Women are often subjected to the belief that showing emotions makes them weak and hindered in achieving success in their careers. However, this perception is flawed and misguided. Far from hindering progress in professional lives, emotions provide unique insights and perspectives that greatly enhance career development. The ability to empathize with others on a deeper level allows women to connect authentically with colleagues and clients alike while understanding complex issues from multiple angles.

Emotional intelligence fosters positive relationships built on empathy and compassion within the workplace environment while also helping them navigate through challenging situations with grace and problem-solving skills rooted in understanding and intuition. By acknowledging and embracing emotions, women tap into a wellspring of creativity, innovation, and resilience that propels their careers and lives forward.

So let us challenge the notion that emotions make us weak. Men should be encouraged to break free from societal expectations that stifle their emotional growth. Women should be empowered to embrace their emotions as sources of strength rather than hindrances to success. Together, we can redefine what it means to be emotionally resilient individuals who value empathy, compassion, and authenticity.

14

Two Sides of The Coin

"Good and bad are like two sides of the same coin"
Dr. Subhas Babu Kode

In life, it's easy to get caught up in the negative aspects of a situation or a person. We tend to focus on what's wrong or what's not going our way, completely disregarding any positives that may be present. However, if we take a moment to step back and look at both sides of the coin, we might just find a different perspective.

Have you ever heard the saying "good and bad are like two sides of the same coin"? It's a great reminder to always look at both sides of a situation or person before making a judgment. It's so easy to focus only on the negative aspects and completely miss the positive ones. But if we take the time to look for the good, we can often find it, even in the most challenging circumstances.

The saying "good and bad are like two sides of the same coin" holds a valuable lesson. It reminds us that before passing judgment, it is crucial to consider all aspects of a situation or person. By doing so, we open ourselves up to understanding and empathy.

Sometimes, it can be challenging to see the positive side of a person when we're feeling down or frustrated. But that's precisely when empathy comes into play. If we make an effort to put ourselves in someone else's shoes and view things from their perspective, we might uncover hidden truths and unexpected positives. Instead of solely focusing on negativity, let's train ourselves to consider both sides of the coin.

The burnt toast theory offers another intriguing perspective on finding silver linings in everyday occurrences. This theory suggests that even irritating or inconvenient events may hold hidden blessings. For instance, burning your toast in the morning might have delayed you enough to avoid getting into a car accident later on your way to work.

While it may seem far-fetched or impossible to determine whether burnt toast genuinely saved you from harm, this theory serves as a gentle reminder: try finding something positive in every situation. Perhaps being stuck in traffic gave you time for personal reflection or catching up on your favorite podcast. Maybe that rainstorm forced you indoors, giving you an opportunity to finish reading that book gathering dust on your shelf.

Life is full of unexpected twists and turns, some more favorable than others. However, by maintaining an open mind and a positive attitude, we can find joy even in the seemingly mundane moments. It's all about shifting our perspective and seeking out the good midst the challenges.

It's essential to remember that good and bad coexist in every situation or person. By choosing to see both sides of the coin, we gain a more well-rounded understanding of the complexities of life. Empathy and understanding play a significant role in this process. Next time you encounter a difficult situation or person, take a moment to flip that coin and examine both sides carefully. You might discover new insights that change your perception entirely.

The concept that there is always another side to everything in life is a profound lesson that has woven its way through generations in my family. My dad learned this valuable insight from his father, my grandpa, who often emphasized the importance of perspective. I remember a particular story my dad shared with me when I was just a small child, around 5 or 6 years old. This is the story:

When my dad was 9 years old, my grandfather took him to one of his friend's house. It so happened that my grandfather's friend indulged in drinking. My dad didn't like this, as he had the preconceived notion that anyone who drank or smoked was a bad person up to no good--a perspective influenced by movies of that time. So, when my grandfather's friend jokingly offered him a glass of whiskey, saying, "Your father doesn't drink anyway. Do you want a drink?" this question/joke enraged my dad. My dad became very offended, and later, when leaving, he asked my grandfather why he was friends with someone he considered a "bad" person.

My grandfather replied, "No, you're mistaken. He is genuinely a good person. You're not able to see this because you're only seeing the negative side. You're unable to see the complete picture. Good and bad are intertwined, much like two sides of a coin. Every individual, including you and me, possess both positive and negative traits; it's impossible to have a coin that features only one side. Always remember that there are many sides to a person or a situation; some will be bad, and some will be good. It's only fair and right that you see both sides of the coin, as one can't exist without the other."

He went on to explain that you will see what you choose to see, and sometimes what you see is not all that there is. You can choose to see only the good or only the bad, but you must see both. When you focus on the good, you will have many friends and a positive outlook on life. When you focus on the bad, you will have "enemies" and a negative outlook. Seeing the good doesn't mean ignoring the bad; it means understanding both sides and choosing to focus on the positive aspects.

This simple yet powerful idea resonated deeply with my dad and has since become a foundational lesson that he has passed down to me. As a young child, I may not have fully grasped the complexities of this concept, but the seeds were planted, and they eventually grew into a way of viewing the world that shaped my understanding of life.

Since that day, the idea of there being two or more sides to every situation has been a constant presence in my thoughts, influencing how I interact with others and approach challenges. It has become the lens through which I view my experiences, allowing me to cultivate patience in moments of frustration and empathy when faced with the struggles of those around me. This single concept has blossomed into a myriad of life lessons, guiding me through various situations. Whether in personal relationships, academic challenges, or everyday decision-making, I find myself reflecting on the different perspectives that exist. The realization that life is rarely black and white has not only enriched my understanding of the world but has also encouraged me to be more compassionate and open-minded.

As we embark on this journey together through the Art of Perception, let us embrace the notion that there is always more than what meets the eye. By honing our ability to see beyond initial impressions, we unlock doors to deeper connections with ourselves and those around us. So let us approach this exploration with curiosity and an unwavering commitment to embracing all sides of every coin we encounter along the way.

"Being positive is not pretending everything is alright, it is seeing the good in everything"
  Unknown

15

Yin and Yang

In life, there exists an intricate balance, where everything seems to have an equal and opposite force. This concept can be seen in the law of nature, where for every action, there is an equal and opposite reaction. It's intriguing to contemplate how this principle applies not only to the realm of physics and science but also to our relationships and emotions.

At times, it may be easy to become consumed by the negative aspects of this balance. We might encounter setbacks or challenges that feel overwhelming. However, it is vital to remember that there is always a counterbalancing force at play. Life resembles a pendulum swinging back and forth; it has its ups and downs but ultimately finds a way to restore equilibrium.

By embracing this natural law of balance, we can learn to appreciate the moments of goodness while maintaining hope during difficult times.

The concept of yin and yang from Chinese philosophy illustrates this harmony between opposing forces in the universe. It signifies that just as light cannot exist without darkness, happiness cannot exist without sadness, and so on. This perspective offers us a beautiful way to perceive the world while seeking harmony in all things.

The idea behind yin and yang reminds me that everything in life is interconnected, allowing the attainment of balance for happiness and fulfillment. It resembles walking on a tightrope—steadiness in avoiding falling off requires practice and mindfulness. Similarly, finding harmony amid opposing forces within our lives allows us to discover inner peace.

It might sound a little bit counterproductive, but isn't it true that we appreciate the good things in life even more when we've experienced some hardships? It's human nature to seek balance, and that's why we need to go through different emotions and situations to truly appreciate what we have. I think it's important to embrace all aspects of life, even the ones that are unpleasant.

Of course, nobody wants to feel sad or go through tough times, but they're a necessary part of our personal growth and development. We learn from our mistakes, we grow stronger from our struggles, and we become more grateful for the good things in life.

So, next time you're feeling down, remember that it's just a temporary state and that better days are ahead. And when those better days come, cherish them and be thankful for every moment.

Karma

Karma is a concept that has been around for centuries, and it refers to the idea that our actions have consequences, both in this life and the next. Essentially, it means that what goes around comes around, and the energy we put out into the world will eventually come back to us in some way.

Some people believe in karma as a spiritual force that governs the universe, while others see it as a simple matter of cause and effect.

I am a firm believer in the concept of karma. It is an incredibly fair system where your actions dictate the results that you experience. If you put out positive energy into the world, good things will come back to you. On the flip side, if you consistently act in a negative manner, you will ultimately face negative consequences. It's a simple but powerful concept that I think everyone can benefit from embracing.

Have you ever heard the saying "You reap what you sow"? Well, that's exactly what karma is all about. It's the idea that the actions we take have consequences, and those consequences will eventually come back to us in some way. I find this concept to be really reassuring because it means that the universe is just and fair. If we're kind and compassionate to others, good things will come our way. On the other hand, if we're cruel or selfish, we'll eventually face the consequences of our actions.

Maybe not immediately but definitely, if not in this life then the next.

Have you ever heard of collective karma? It's a fascinating concept that suggests that the actions and deeds of a group, whether it be a family, community, or even a nation, can influence the future experiences of its members. The idea is that every action we take, every thought we have, and every word we speak creates an energy that affects not only ourselves but also those around us. This energy can accumulate over time and shape the collective karma of a group. So, it's essential to be mindful of our actions and their potential impact on those around us. By doing so, we can contribute to creating positive karma and improve the lives of those in our family and communities.

While it's not a proven scientific theory, it's interesting to consider how our actions and attitudes can impact not just our own lives, but the lives of those around us as well.

Regardless of how you view karma, it's important to remember that the choices we make and the actions we take can have a profound impact on ourselves and those around us. By striving to do good and make positive contributions to the world, we can create a ripple effect of positivity that can spread far and wide.

So let's all try to be the best versions of ourselves and practice kindness, compassion, and generosity whenever possible. Who knows, maybe our good deeds will come back to us in ways we never could have imagined!

16

The Art of Empathy

"Empathy is about finding echoes of another person in yourself"
Moshin Hamid

In a world that often feels disconnected, cultivating empathy is more crucial than ever. Empathy is the core of human connection, allowing us to bridge gaps and build deeper relationships. It's not just about acknowledging others' emotions but genuinely experiencing them ourselves. To truly empathize, we must step out of our own perspective and immerse ourselves in someone else's experience, requiring both an open mind and a sincere desire to support others.

While empathy might come more naturally to some, everyone can develop it with effort. However, regardless of where we fall on the empathy spectrum, it is crucial to remember that empathy is not just about thinking or feeling but also about caring. Empathy means listening with our hearts and responding with genuine concern, not merely offering superficial words or gestures.

On the flip side, indifference can be seen as the absence of empathy – a lack of concern for others' feelings and experiences. Being indifferent goes beyond not caring or lacking interest; it is a state of mind where we do not have any strong preference or bias towards a particular outcome or situation.

In a world that is becoming increasingly self-centered and consumed by technology, it is easy to fall into the trap of indifference. Our excessive screen time and obsession with social media often leads us to disregard or dismiss those who hold different opinions than ours, resulting in a lack of empathy and hindered connections.

In today's fast-paced world, it is not uncommon to find ourselves becoming indifferent due to the overwhelming amount of information and distractions around us. However, it is important to recognize that indifference can have negative consequences on our relationships and personal growth.

As we become more absorbed in our own lives and social media, we may unintentionally neglect the importance of understanding and connecting with others.

But, by consciously acknowledging and challenging our own indifference, we open ourselves up to a world of personal growth and learning. Embracing diverse perspectives allows us to expand our knowledge and understanding of the world around us. It gives us the chance to develop empathy and compassion for others, fostering stronger and more meaningful connections.

Instead of shutting ourselves off from different opinions, we should strive to engage in open and respectful dialogue. Recognizing the value in hearing and considering alternative viewpoints not only broadens our own horizons but also contributes to a more inclusive and harmonious society.

Embracing empathy as an art form involves practice, patience, and genuine care. By doing so, we foster a world where human connections flourish, understanding replaces judgment, and compassion triumphs over indifference.

From a young age, I've always had a natural tendency towards empathy, but my dad played a crucial role in nurturing that trait as I grew up. One of my earliest memories that truly showcased this was when I faced a tough choice: I could either watch a movie I had been eagerly anticipating for weeks or help two tiny rabbits. We had come across a man selling these baby rabbits by the roadside, and they were so small they resembled little eggs. My heart ached for them, thinking about how they were separated from their mother and thrust into a life of uncertainty. The sight of those fragile creatures stirred something profound within me, and I felt a compelling urge to take action, to alleviate their suffering in whatever way I could.

As I voiced my concerns to my dad he recognized how deeply I felt about the situation. He proposed a deal: I could adopt the rabbits if I chose to forego the movie and use that money to buy their freedom. In that moment, I grappled with the choice before me--an evening of entertainment that I had looked forward to for so long versus the chance to save two innocent lives. Looking back, I realize that while I was excited at the thought of having adorable rabbits as pets, my desire to rescue them was driven by a deeper wish to provide them with the love and freedom they deserved. My dad's support in that decision not only reinforced my empathy but also taught me the importance of making sacrifices for those who cannot speak for themselves. That day, I learned that true fulfillment often comes from acts of kindness, and the joy of giving was far greater than any fleeting pleasure I could have found in a movie theater.

Those rabbits went on to live for ten wonderful years, filling my life with joy and warmth. Each day was an adventure as they explored their surroundings, their twitching noses and soft fur always reminding me of the simple pleasures in life. I would often find them basking in the sun, their little bodies stretching out in contentment, or playfully chasing each other around the garden. Treats became a daily ritual, whether it was fresh vegetables or the occasional piece of fruit, and their delighted antics as they nibbled away at their snacks brought a smile to my face. As time went on, they also welcomed little ones into the world, and witnessing the miracle of new life was nothing short of enchanting. It was a constant reminder of the cycle of life and the joy that comes with nurturing and caring for those we love.

Caring for my rabbits taught me invaluable lessons about empathy, responsibility, and love--lessons that extended far beyond the confines of their hutch. Each rabbit had its own unique personality, and learning to understand their individual needs and quirks required patience and attentiveness. I found myself becoming more attuned to the emotions of others, realizing that just like my furry companions, everyone has their own ways of expressing feelings and seeking comfort. The responsibility of their care instilled a sense of discipline in me; I learned to prioritize their well-being over my own desires, such as skipping a movie night to ensure they were fed and happy. Looking back, I have no regrets about missing that movie. The connection I forged with my rabbits was far more rewarding, and if given the chance, I would make that same choice over and over again, knowing that the love and companionship we shared created memories that would last a lifetime.

* * *

Sympathy vs. Empathy

Empathy goes beyond sympathy. While sympathy involves feeling sorry for someone's struggles from a distance, empathy requires immersing ourselves in their emotional experience. Empathy demands vulnerability and active listening, allowing us to connect deeply with others without judgment.

Empathetic individuals recognize the universality of human experiences while honoring individual differences. They understand that pain is not confined by boundaries such as race or social status and offer support. Empathy encourages dialogue and compassion, transforming relationships and communities.

Incorporating empathy in leadership and personal interactions can lead to decisions that prioritize human well-being over personal gain. It extends inwardly as well, allowing us to navigate our own emotions with kindness and understanding.

Empathic Listening

"Listening is about being present, not just quiet"
  Krista Tippet

Empathic listening is more than hearing words; it's about being fully present, engaging with emotions and body language, and avoiding interruptions. It requires setting aside our own judgments and biases to create an environment where the speaker feels heard and validated.

Practicing empathic listening involves genuine curiosity and openness, focusing on understanding rather than steering the conversation toward our own experiences. This skill deepens connections and fosters trust, enhancing our relationships.

I used to be a terrible listener when I was younger. Caught up in my own thoughts and eager to share my own side of things, I often overlooked the importance of truly hearing others. However, my dad has always been an exceptional listener. Throughout my life, he has been there for countless rants and vent sessions, making me feel truly heard and understood.

One day, my dad shared a story about fate that deeply resonated with me. He explained that every person we encounter in life is meant to be in our path for a reason - whether they are just passing by or become lifelong friends. These interactions are all destined, and it's up to us to fully embrace and appreciate the experience of being with them.

According to my dad's philosophy, there is always something valuable to learn from everyone we meet along our journey through life. Each person brings their own unique experiences and perspectives that can enrich our understanding of the world around us. It's not just about exchanging words; it's about sharing our entire presence and being with one another.
This exchange or connection between individuals is what makes life beautiful; it allows us to grow as individuals while also contributing something meaningful to someone else's life.

My dad's words have stayed with me over the years as a
constant reminder of how important it is to truly listen and
be present in every interaction.

As I grew older, I gradually learned how to become a better
listener. I realized that my dad's words were more than just
advice; they were a profound insight into the power of
empathic listening. I began to understand that being fully
present in conversations not only deepens our understanding
of others but also allows us to connect on a much deeper
level.

When we practice empathic listening, it is important to remember
that "it's not about you." It's not about proving ourselves right or
imposing our own opinions onto others. Instead, it's about creating an
environment where the speaker feels heard, validated, and understood.

Empathic listening is an art that requires practice and intentionality. By
fully embracing this skill, we can deepen our connections with others
and foster meaningful relationships based on trust and understanding.
Let us remember my dad's words: 'every interaction is meant to teach
us something valuable if we are open to receiving it.' So let us embrace
the power of true listening - for ourselves and for those around us - as
we continue on this journey of perception.

Empathy vs Indifference

Empathy and indifference are opposing choices. Empathy is a conscious decision to connect deeply with others, whereas indifference acts
as a shield against potential pain and discomfort. Choosing empathy

over indifference fosters personal growth and opens us up to new perspectives and connections.

When we embrace empathy over indifference, we become more receptive to different ideas and compassionate towards others. It transforms us into agents of positive change, enabling us to make a meaningful difference in the world. By choosing empathy, we contribute to a more understanding and compassionate society.

In every interaction, practice empathy by setting aside preconceived notions and seeking to understand others genuinely. The rewards of empathy enrich both our lives and the lives of those around us, creating a world where people feel seen, heard, and valued.

As we choose empathy over indifference, we become agents of change. Our ability to understand and connect with others on a deeper level empowers us to make a positive difference in the world.

Let us remember that empathy does not require us to experience everything firsthand—it simply asks us to extend kindness, compassion, and understanding towards others. By choosing empathy in our daily interactions, we contribute to a collective shift towards a more empathetic world—one where people feel seen, heard, and understood.

The Art of Compassion

"If you want others to be happy, practice compassion. If you want to be happy, practice compassion." — Dalai Lama XIV

These words spoken by the Dalai Lama hold great meaning and

significance. Compassion is often underestimated, but it goes beyond being just a word.

Compassion goes beyond mere emotional response; it is an intentional practice that shapes how we engage with the world. At its core, compassion means recognizing others' suffering and taking steps to alleviate it. It connects our hearts to others, fostering deeper understanding and mutual respect.

To practice compassion, start by nurturing it within yourself. Acknowledge your own vulnerabilities and challenges, which helps you relate to others' experiences. Compassion begins with self-awareness and extends outward, forming the basis for genuine empathetic connections.

"if your compassion doesn't include yourself it is incomplete"
Buddha

Effective compassion involves active listening and being present. It's more than feeling sympathy; it requires engaging deeply, offering a non-judgmental ear, and validating others' feelings. By listening closely, you build trust and connection.

Compassion also means taking action, whether through offering comforting words, practical help, or simply being there for someone in need. The goal is to show care and support, even with small gestures.

Remember, compassion is a two-way street. While being compassionate is vital, accepting other's compassion towards us gracefully also strengthens relationships and fosters mutual respect.

Ultimately, compassion enriches both our lives and those we encounter. It transforms interactions into meaningful connections and enhances emotional resilience. Compassion is a continuous practice, enriching our world one act of kindness at a time.

Compassion has always been a guiding force in my life, largely thanks to my dad, who truly embodied kindness in every aspect of his existence. Whether he was addressing minor inconveniences or grappling with significant challenges, his approach remained steadfast: he treated everyone with respect and empathy. His mantra, "You lose nothing by being compassionate, but you gain everything," was not merely a saying; it was a principle he lived by daily. It was through him that I learned the true essence of compassion--not just feeling for others but taking tangible steps to alleviate their suffering. His unwavering belief in the power of compassion instilled in me a desire to embody these values in my own life.

My understanding of compassion deepened significantly through the experience of rescuing my dogs with the help of my dad. Each rescue journey served as a humbling reminder of the harsh realities many animals endure, often neglected or abandoned. The transformation of these dogs--from fearful and anxious creatures to joyful and secure companions--was a testament to the healing power of love and kindness. These experiences have taught me that compassion knows no bounds and can make a profound difference in the lives of the most vulnerable. My dogs mean the world to me, and every wag of their tails serves as a reminder of how far a little kindness can go, reinforcing my belief that compassion is not just an act; it is a way of life that enriches both the giver and the receiver.

Empathy vs Compassion

Empathy and compassion are often used interchangeably, they represent distinct interconnected aspects of human connection. Understanding both concepts and how they complement each other can deepen our relationships and enhance our ability to support others.

Empathy is the capacity to deeply understand and share another person's emotions, essentially stepping into their shoes and experiencing their feelings as if they were your own. This emotional resonance helps build strong, personal connections by allowing us to relate to others on a profound level.

Compassion, however, goes a step further. It encompasses not only the understanding of another's suffering, as empathy does, but also involves a proactive response aimed at alleviating that suffering. While empathy creates a bridge of emotional connection, compassion turns that connection into meaningful action. It involves actively providing support, comfort, or assistance to address the needs of others. Thus, while empathy helps us connect on an emotional plane, compassion transforms that connection into tangible efforts to improve someone's situation.

As we conclude this exploration of empathy, compassion, and their profound impacts on our lives, it's clear that these virtues are essential for fostering meaningful connections in a fragmented world.

Empathy, the art of finding echoes of another person's experience within ourselves, allows us to bridge gaps and build deeper relationships by truly understanding and sharing in others' emotions.

Compassion extends this connection by inspiring us to take action, offering support and alleviating the suffering we perceive. Both empathy and compassion require conscious effort, intentional practice, and an open heart.

By embracing these qualities, we can transform our interactions, enrich our personal growth, and contribute to a more connected and compassionate society. Let us remember that each act of empathy and compassion ripples outward, creating a world where everyone feels seen, heard, and valued.

17

The Art of Humility

"Pride will always have it's consequences, humility will always
have it's reward"
  Unknown

Humility is a profound strength that enables us to view ourselves and others with both clarity and grace. It is the quality of acknowledging our own limitations while appreciating and valuing the contributions of those around us. At its core, humility involves recognizing that our achievements are often intertwined with the collective efforts of others, and that no success is solely our own. This understanding shifts our focus from seeking excessive praise or validation to embracing the broader context in which we operate.

Contrary to the misconception that humility equates to self-deprecation or undervaluing oneself, true humility is about maintaining a balanced perspective. It involves accepting our imperfections and mistakes with openness, seeing them as opportunities for growth rather than as personal failings. By embracing humility, we allow ourselves the space to continually learn and improve, fostering a mindset that welcomes constructive feedback and collaborative efforts. This approach helps us avoid the pitfalls of arrogance and entitlement, which can undermine relationships and hinder personal development.

In our interactions and relationships, humility manifests as a deep respect for others. It means actively listening with an open mind, genuinely considering diverse viewpoints, and acknowledging the worth of others' experiences and opinions. This respectful attitude not only nurtures trust and harmony but also creates the foundation for more meaningful and effective connections. When we approach others with humility, we foster an environment where mutual understanding and cooperation can thrive.

Ultimately, humility enriches our perception of the world by encouraging us to approach each situation with an open heart and a receptive mind. It helps us navigate life's challenges with grace and fosters deeper, more authentic relationships. By practicing humility, we contribute to a culture of mutual respect and understanding, enhancing our ability to connect with others in a profound and genuine way. In essence, humility is not just a personal virtue but a vital component of building a more empathetic and harmonious world.

Humility is a remarkable trait that holds the power to transform our lives. It is the quality of being modest, unassuming, and not seeking recognition for our accomplishments. Individuals who embody humility are not solely focused on themselves but instead make choices that positively impact those around them. They possess an inner confidence that doesn't require constant validation or boasting about their achievements.

Contrary to popular belief, humility is not about thinking less of oneself but rather thinking about oneself less. When we embrace humility, we naturally show respect to others and understand the importance of relying on friends, family, and colleagues for support.

In a world that often encourages showmanship and self-promotion, it can be easy to lose sight of the true value of humility. But those who possess this virtue understand its immense power in fostering genuine connections and creating a harmonious environment around them.

As I reflect on my journey into adulthood, I recall one particular lesson my father imparted upon me a lesson rooted in humility. At eighteen years old, stepping into the financial world was both exhilarating and daunting. There were so many lessons yet to be learned, so many pitfalls waiting to ensnare me. However, armed with my father's wisdom, I had faith that I wouldn't lose sight of what truly matters - living a fulfilling life.
The concept he taught me was having an abundance mindset - an approach that defies scarcity mentality by recognizing the vast opportunities available in this world. It goes hand in hand with humility because it reminds us that there is enough wealth and happiness for everyone; it's not limited or finite.

An abundance mindset encourages us to celebrate others' achievements instead of feeling threatened by them. It urges us to collaborate rather than compete because we know there is room for all of us to thrive. It allows us to let go of jealousy and envy, replacing them with genuine happiness for others' accomplishments.

As I continue on my financial journey, I hold onto this lesson tightly. With an abundance mindset, I am confident that I can build wealth and success without losing sight of

the values that truly matter. It reminds me to remain humble
in the face of prosperity and to resist the temptation of
arrogance.
Humility in our financial pursuits is not about downplaying
our achievements or denying ourselves celebration. Rather,
it is about approaching success with grace and gratitude. It
is about recognizing that our accomplishments are not solely
due to our own efforts but are often a result of the support
and guidance we receive from others along the way.
As I go through life, I choose humility as my guiding
principle because it aligns with who I want to be as a
person - someone grounded, compassionate, and always aware
of the impact my actions have on those around me.

Ancient Indian scriptures, including texts such as the Ramayana, Bhagavad Gita and the Vedas, profoundly emphasize the importance of humility as a cornerstone of one's character and spiritual growth. Humility is portrayed not merely as a passive quality but as an active virtue.

Lord Rama's first task from his teacher, Vashishtha, was to go out and beg for food (bhikkshatana). Although Rama was a prince, being the son of King Dashratha, his guru believed it was important for him to practice humility. Vashishtha wanted Rama to learn to let go of any sense of entitlement and embrace a more grounded perspective.

Buddha also emphasizes the significance of humility in both personal and communal living, highlighting it as a key virtue on the path to enlightenment. This principle of humility is deeply rooted in Buddhist teachings, where the act of letting go of ego and self-importance is seen as essential for spiritual growth.

One practical manifestation of this teaching can be observed in the lifestyle of Buddhist monks, who often rely on the generosity of others for their sustenance. By accepting donations instead of seeking wealth or forming attachments to material possessions, monks embody humility and foster a sense of interconnectedness with their community. Relying on alms not only reinforces their commitment to simplicity and detachment but also encourages other people to engage in acts of kindness and generosity, thereby enhancing the communal bonds that supports spiritual development.

So let us strive for humility in all aspects of our lives - not just financially but also in our relationships, careers, and personal growth. Let us remember that true power lies not in dominating others but rather in lifting them up.

18

The Art of Giving

"For it is in giving we receive"
St.Francis of Assisi

The art of giving is a tapestry woven from threads of generosity, empathy, and selflessness. It is a practice deeply embedded in the human experience, transcending cultures, beliefs, and boundaries. Giving is not merely a transaction of exchanging something of value; it is a profound expression of connection and humanity. Whether through gifts, time, knowledge, or presence, the true essence of giving lies in the purity of intention and the depth of sincerity behind each gesture.

There are many forms of giving here are some examples...

Gifts are often the most tangible form of giving. From a carefully chosen present on a special occasion to a spontaneous gesture of kindness, gifts serve as physical manifestations of our thoughts and feelings. Yet, the value of a gift is not defined by its cost but by the sentiment it conveys. A handmade card, a book shared with a friend, or a simple bouquet of flowers can carry profound meaning and show how much we care.

The art of gift-giving goes beyond the act of handing over an object. It involves understanding the recipient's needs and desires, reflecting on their preferences, and selecting something that resonates with them. A well-chosen gift demonstrates attentiveness and thoughtfulness, turning a simple exchange into a memorable experience. For example, a thoughtful gift for someone going through a tough time could be a carefully curated care package filled with their favorite comfort items—showing empathy and understanding beyond words.

In a world that moves at a relentless pace, time has become one of the most precious things you could ever give to someone. Giving someone your time is a profound expression of love and respect. Whether it's sitting down for a heartfelt conversation, helping a friend through a difficult period, or simply spending quality moments with loved ones, time is a gift that conveys our prioritization of their presence in our lives.

The value of time is evident in the way it fosters deeper connections. When we invest our time in someone, we are demonstrating that they matter to us more than our own convenience. Imagine a parent attending their child's school play, despite a busy schedule, or a friend dropping everything to support a loved one in need. These acts of devotion illustrate the power of giving our time, strengthening bonds and creating lasting memories.

Knowledge is a gift with the power to transform lives in meaningful ways. When we share what we know—whether through teaching, mentoring, or advising—we extend more than just a collection of facts;

we offer a gateway to growth and success. The act of giving knowledge is deeply enriching because it involves nurturing curiosity, igniting passion, and instilling confidence in others. Imagine a teacher who doesn't just deliver a lesson but instead inspires students to explore their interests and think critically, sparking a lifelong love for learning. Or consider a mentor who, through years of experience, guides a young professional not only with strategic advice but also by modeling resilience and leadership. This kind of giving is about fostering an environment where individuals feel empowered to push their boundaries and realize their potential. It is about creating opportunities for personal and professional development that can significantly impact a person's trajectory. Sharing knowledge, therefore, is an investment in the future—both of the individuals we help and the broader community they will influence. In doing so, we contribute to a cycle of continuous learning and improvement that benefits everyone involved.

Presence is perhaps the most subtle yet impactful form of giving. It involves being mentally and emotionally available for others, offering them our full attention and support. True presence requires us to set aside our own distractions and immerse ourselves fully in the moment with someone else.

Imagine a friend who listens with genuine empathy during a challenging conversation or a partner who is entirely engaged during a meaningful discussion. Their presence is a gift that fosters trust and connection, creating an environment where open communication and understanding can flourish. Being present shows that we value the other person's feelings and experiences, enhancing the depth of our relationships.

Always remember that the true essence of giving lies in the purity of our intentions. It is crucial to approach giving without expecting anything in return or feeling entitled. When we give with an agenda or anticipate a reward, we taint the act of giving with conditions and expectations. The art of giving is diminished when it becomes a means to an end rather than an expression of genuine care and compassion.

For instance, consider a situation where someone donates money to a charity but expects public recognition or praise in return. The act of giving, in this case, is overshadowed by the desire for validation, detracting from the true purpose of supporting a cause. Conversely, giving without expectation—whether it's through charitable contributions, acts of kindness, or support for loved ones—nurtures a spirit of generosity that is both meaningful and fulfilling.

Giving is an intrinsic part of what it means to be human. From ancient rituals to modern practices, the act of giving has always been central to our interactions and relationships. It is a fundamental aspect of our social fabric, promoting empathy, cooperation, and mutual respect.

By giving thoughtfully and without attachment to outcomes, we honor the true spirit of generosity. Whether through gifts, time, knowledge, or presence, the act of giving enriches our lives and the lives of those around us.

In conclusion, the art of giving is a celebration of our shared humanity. It is a practice that, when approached with sincerity and compassion, enhances our relationships, fosters community, and reflects the best of who we are. As we navigate our lives, let us remember that the most meaningful gifts are those given with a pure heart—free from expectations and filled with genuine love and care. In this way, we contribute to a world where giving becomes a powerful force for connection, understanding, and shared joy.

I am a product of all those who came before me, in more ways
than one. For generations, my family has embraced the spirit
of giving--whether it's love, time, or kindness. My
great-grandfather was a remarkable man known for his
generosity; he would always go above and beyond to help
anyone in need, often giving back much more than he
received. This selfless nature was instilled in my
grandmother, who embodies the essence of a giver. She has
always been overflowing with love and is constantly finding
reasons to give gifts, a trait she's had since her youth.

My father inherited this same spirit, being thoughtful with
his words and actions. He taught me not just how to give the
best gifts, but also the true art of giving itself. Today,
giving is an integral part of who I am, enriching my life
and the lives of those around me. It's not always about
grand gestures; sometimes, it's the small acts of kindness
that make the biggest impact.

Giver vs Receiver

In our society, there is a tendency to place the giver on a pedestal, showering them with accolades and admiration. Conversely, those in need of help are often looked down upon. This societal bias has led many of us to strive to be givers rather than receivers.

But let us pause for a moment and examine this stereotypical thinking. In order to create truly beautiful moments of generosity, both the giver and the receiver are equally necessary. When someone reaches out for help, our natural response should be one of giving, without critically analyzing their needs or worthiness.

An essential aspect of giving is that it should never be based on who the recipient is. Giving should flow from within us as a natural response, free from judgments or evaluations. We must not position ourselves as judges of someone's situation because in doing so, we elevate ourselves above them. In reality, both the giver and receiver hold equal standing in this transaction; neither can exist without the other.

When we embrace the role of receiver, we allow others to experience the joy that comes from giving wholeheartedly. By accepting help graciously, we honor not only their generosity but also their desire to connect with us on a deeper level. It takes strength and humility to be open to receiving assistance when needed.

Similarly, being a giver requires more than just material offerings; it demands an open heart and mind as well. True giving involves seeing beyond surface-level judgments or preconceived notions about others' worthiness. It means recognizing that everyone has inherent value regardless of their circumstances.

In our quest to become better givers, we must strive to cultivate a genuine sense of empathy and compassion. By doing so, we create an environment where giving becomes a natural response, devoid of hesitation or skepticism. We shift our focus from evaluating the receiver's worthiness to embracing the opportunity to make a positive impact in someone's life.

It is crucial to remember that generosity goes beyond material possessions or financial assistance. Sometimes, the most meaningful gifts we can offer are intangible—our time, attention, and emotional support. A listening ear or a comforting presence can be more valuable than any tangible item.

As we navigate the delicate dance between giving and receiving, let us release ourselves from societal expectations and embrace the inherent beauty in both roles. Recognize that being a giver does not make us superior; it simply allows us to contribute our unique strengths and resources. Likewise, being a receiver does not diminish our worth; it grants others the opportunity to experience the joy of giving.

True generosity lies in finding harmony between giving and receiving. It requires us to let go of judgments and embrace both roles with humility and grace.

When we approach acts of giving with an Open heart and mind while accepting help with gratitude and appreciation, we create a world where kindness flows freely—a world where both givers and receivers thrive together in harmony.

III

Part Three

UNDERSTANDING LIFE

19

Living in the Moment

Many of us find it difficult to truly live in the moment. It's easy to get caught up in the past or worry about the future, but it's important to take a step back and appreciate the present. As Oogway from Kung Fu Panda wisely said:

> "Yesterday is history, tomorrow is a mystery, but today is a gift; that is why we call it the present."

This quote resonates deeply because it reminds us of the preciousness of each moment. Never let the sadness of your past and the fear of your future ruin your happiness in the present. It's unfortunate that we often become so preoccupied with what was and what will be that we forget to live fully in the here and now. Living in the moment means fully immersing yourself in now. It means letting go of regrets from the past and worries about the future, and instead focusing on appreciating all that exists at this very moment.

Imagine a sunny day at the beach - feeling warmth caress your skin, listening to waves crash against shorelines, breathing in salty sea air. In that moment, there's no room for thoughts about yesterday's mistakes or tomorrow's uncertainties. You are simply there – fully present and alive. Living in this way allows you to cherish even life's smallest joys and find beauty everywhere.

It's like savoring a delicious meal; you take time to enjoy each bite, relishing flavors and textures. This approach should extend beyond meals; it should permeate our entire lives – through mindfulness, gratitude, and wonderment.

So next time you find yourself dwelling on past events or worrying incessantly about what lies ahead, remember to come back to this very moment - take a deep breath - look around you - be grateful for this gift called now. Life unfolds right here before our eyes; don't miss out on its magic by getting lost in thoughts that don't serve you.

My dad always used to say, "Nothing is forever," and it took me a while to truly grasp its meaning. He would remind me that we won't always be together, so we should make the most of every moment and treasure the time we have. Initially, this notion scared me; I feared losing those I loved. However, as time passed, I realized that my father's words were not meant to instill fear but rather to awaken an awareness of life's fleeting nature.

Each moment is unique and transient, making it incredibly precious. Instead of dreading the passage of time, I learned to view it as a gift — a reminder to fully engage in every moment without dwelling on the past or fretting about the future. While worries occasionally crept into my thoughts, I made a conscious effort not to let them overshadow my daily life.

Living in the present requires practice and intentionality. It means letting go of regrets that weigh us down and embracing the possibilities that lie before us right now. It means being fully present for ourselves and for those around us.

When you live in the moment, you bring your entire self into everything you do – your mind is clear, your senses are heightened, and your heart is open. You experience life more deeply because you are fully engaged with what is happening right now.

By living in the present moment, we can cultivate gratitude for all that surrounds us - even during challenging times when finding joy seems impossible. We start recognizing beauty in simple things: a sunrise painting colors across the sky or laughter shared with loved ones.

"The most beautiful moments in life were moments when you were not thinking about anything. You were just living"
Sadhguru

Living in the moment allows us to release unnecessary burdens from our pasts and free ourselves from anxieties about what may come tomorrow. It invites us to fully embrace our lives as they are unfolding right now - imperfectly perfect.

So let us take this wisdom to heart - learn from Oogway and my father - and choose to live in the present. Let us appreciate the gift of now, for it is all we truly have. In doing so, we can unlock a world of joy, gratitude, and fulfillment that awaits us in every passing moment.

The Art of Contentment

"He is richest who is content with the least, for content is the
wealth of nature"
   Socrates

In the pursuit of happiness, we often overlook the power of contentment. While happiness can be fleeting and dependent on external
factors, contentment is a state of mind that can be sustained even in
difficult circumstances. It allows us to find joy in the present moment
and appreciate what we already have.

Being content with oneself is one of the most valuable achievements
in life. It does not require perfection or having everything we desire;
rather, it involves finding happiness and fulfillment in the present
moment. When we are content, we can focus on our goals and
aspirations without comparing ourselves to others or dwelling on
past mistakes. However, finding contentment is not always easy –
it requires self-reflection and a willingness to let go of the need to
compare yourself with others.

One way to cultivate contentment is by practicing gratitude. By
focusing on the things we are grateful for, we shift our perspective
from what we lack to what we have. This mindset helps us appreciate
even the simplest things in life and find joy in them. Additionally,
prioritizing self-care plays a crucial role in cultivating contentment.
Taking care of our physical, mental, and emotional well-being enables
us to find inner peace and fulfillment.

It's essential to understand that contentment is not a destination but a journey. Life consists of ups and downs, but embracing both with trust in our own strength allows us to navigate through them successfully. The ability to find contentment amidst challenges grants us resilience and empowers us to face any obstacle that comes our way.

While happiness is often considered as the key to success, I argue that being content holds even greater power. Contentment allows us to sustain a positive state of mind regardless of external circumstances – it frees us from constantly searching for something more or better. By appreciating what we have and finding joy in the present moment, we experience inner peace and fulfillment. This mindset can then lead to greater success in all areas of life.

If you find yourself stressed or unsatisfied with where you are in life, I encourage you to shift your focus towards finding contentment in the present moment. By doing so, you may discover that it positively impacts your overall well-being. Embracing contentment allows us to navigate through challenges with resilience, gratitude, and optimism.

Finding contentment does not mean being fully satisfied with our current life situation. Instead, it involves recognizing and appreciating our present circumstances while acknowledging the progress we have made thus far. It is about embracing the journey ahead wholeheartedly – a journey filled with both beauty and imperfections.

Contentment invites us to shift our focus from what has gone wrong to what has gone right; from what we lack to what we have. By cultivating gratitude and optimism, we can navigate life's ups and downs with a lighter heart. Remember that contentment is not about reaching a final destination of perfection but rather about finding peace and fulfillment within the journey itself.

Finding contentment often also stems from embracing simplicity. Living with simplicity is a conscious choice that many people are beginning to embrace in our fast-paced, consumer-driven world. At its core, simplicity is about reducing the clutter in our lives—both physical and mental—to make room for what truly matters. This approach often involves decluttering our living spaces, letting go of items that no longer serve a purpose or bring us joy, and instead focusing on quality over quantity. By surrounding ourselves with fewer possessions, we can create an environment that fosters peace and mindfulness. This practice extends beyond our physical surroundings; it also invites us to simplify our schedules and commitments, allowing for more time to engage in meaningful relationships and activities that nourish our souls.

Simple living doesn't mean leading a life devoid of enjoyment or excitement. Instead, it encourages us to find joy in the little things, such as a quiet morning with a cup of coffee, a stroll in nature, or a heartfelt conversation with a friend. It invites us to be more intentional about our choices—whether that's in what we consume, how we spend our time, or the relationships we cultivate. Embracing simplicity can lead to a more content and mindful life, where we prioritize experiences and connections over material possessions. Ultimately, it is about creating a lifestyle that aligns with our values, allowing us to appreciate the beauty in everyday moments while fostering a deeper sense of gratitude for what we have.

Take a moment now to appreciate how far you've come on your unique path. Look forward to all the possibilities that lie ahead while embracing the beauty of your journey. As you continue on this path of living in the moment and cultivating contentment, trust that it will guide you towards a more fulfilling and meaningful life experience.

Contentment holds immense power in our lives. It allows us to find joy in the simplest things, appreciate what we have, and navigate through challenges with resilience and optimism. Cultivating contentment is an ongoing process that requires self-reflection, gratitude, and prioritizing self-care. So embrace this beautiful journey of finding peace within yourself as you continue on your path towards living in the moment – for therein lies true fulfillment.

20

The Best Place in Life

Have you ever found yourself daydreaming about the "greener grass" on the other side? It's a common expression we use to express our longing for something we don't have. We often believe that others have it better than us – better jobs, better relationships, and overall happiness.

Our perception is often skewed by our desires and insecurities. In our minds, we tend to idealize what we don't possess and overlook the challenges that others may be facing. We create this illusion of a perfect life on the other side, where everything is easy and filled with joy. However, reality tells a different story.

Every person, situation, and circumstance comes with its own set of challenges. What may seem like greener grass is often just a different shade of green with its own patches of dryness and weeds.

When we constantly compare ourselves to others and focus on what we lack, we fail to appreciate the beauty and opportunities that exist in our own lives.

It's effortless to idealize someone else's situation while only seeing the surface level. We forget that everyone has their struggles and insecurities. What appears as "greener grass" from a distance may not be as perfect as it seems once you get closer.

Instead of longing for what we don't have, let us shift our perspective to appreciate and nurture the grass right beneath our feet – right here, right now.

When we focus on appreciating what's already in front of us rather than coveting what others possess, something magical happens – gratitude blossoms within us. We start noticing all the blessings surrounding us – big or small – that make life truly meaningful.

For instance, take a moment to reflect on your job - maybe it isn't your dream career or even close to it, but are there aspects of it that bring you joy? Perhaps it's the supportive colleagues, the opportunities for personal growth, or the sense of stability it provides. By finding gratitude in these elements, we can transform our perception and find fulfillment even in seemingly mundane tasks.

Similarly, when it comes to relationships, we often look at others and idealize their seemingly perfect partnerships. But what about your own connections? Are there moments of love and support shared between you and your loved ones that fill your heart with warmth? Cherish those moments; they are the building blocks of strong bonds.

By shifting our focus from what we lack to what we have, we unlock a newfound appreciation for our own lives. We begin to see that while the grass may appear greener on the other side, true happiness lies in nurturing and tending to our own patch of grass.

When we water our grass with gratitude and self-compassion, it flourishes. We realize that every opportunity for growth and fulfillment is within reach if only we embrace the present moment wholeheartedly.

Let me reiterate there is no point in getting caught up in the idea that others have it better, when the truth is that we have to face our own reality right now. We can't change our circumstances or where we are in life at this moment. If we're constantly focused on what's next or what we lack, we risk overlooking the value of what we already have. If there's nothing you can do about a situation in the next five minutes, it's probably best to let it go and focus on the present.

We all have to navigate life with the cards we're dealt. It's not helpful to waste time envying others, assuming they have it better, especially since we can't truly know their situation or change our own. What we can do is focus on making the most of what we have and develop a strategy to play our hand as effectively as possible.

So let us not be swayed by illusions that others have it better but instead cultivate an unyielding love for ourselves and our lives just as they are. Our grass may not be flawless or without patches of dryness, but its imperfections make it uniquely ours – a testament to resilience and growth.

* * *

In this fast-paced world, it's easy to get caught up in the hustle and bustle of everyday life. We often find ourselves longing for what lies ahead or reminiscing about what has passed. But amidst all this chaos, there is a profound truth that we often overlook - the best place to be in life is exactly where you are, right here, right now.

Why is being present so important? Because in this very moment, you have the opportunity to fully embrace and appreciate all aspects of your life. Every experience, every struggle, every triumph has contributed to shaping you into the person you are today. From the highest of highs to the lowest of lows, you have witnessed your own growth and resilience.

This perspective was shared with me by my father who believed that we encounter specific moments in life because our souls have lessons to learn and experiences to gain. Each moment serves as a stepping stone towards fulfilling our innermost desires and needs. Even when faced with adversity or sadness, I find solace in knowing that there is something valuable to take away from it all. Perhaps I will emerge from these challenges stronger and wiser than before.

Moreover, being fully present allows for self-reflection and personal growth. It provides an opportunity for us to assess our current situation and identify areas for improvement. By acknowledging and accepting where we are in life, we can tap into our full potential and make positive changes that will propel us forward.

This journey of self-discovery begins with understanding our strengths and weaknesses. When we know what we excel at, we can leverage those skills to pursue opportunities that align with our passions and abilities. However, it's equally important to recognize our weaknesses as they present an opportunity for growth and improvement.

By embracing where we are right now - strengths included - we open ourselves up to a world of possibilities. We can make informed decisions, set realistic goals, and navigate life's twists and turns with confidence and resilience. This self-awareness becomes the foundation upon which our future is built.

But being present doesn't mean we should become complacent. It's essential to be proactive in our personal development by continuously seeking growth opportunities. By cultivating new skills and uncovering hidden talents, we expand our horizons and unlock doors that were once closed to us.

So, I urge you to embrace the present moment with open arms. Allow yourself to fully experience life as it unfolds before you. Take a moment to reflect on your journey - the highs, the lows, and everything in between. Recognize the valuable lessons each experience has taught you.

In this very moment lies immense power - the power to shape your future, the power to create lasting change, and most importantly, the power to find fulfillment right where you are. So let go of regrets from the past and worries about the future. Embrace this present moment for all its beauty and potential.

For it is in this very moment that you have everything you need - all the strength, wisdom, and resilience required to navigate any challenges that come your way. The best place in life truly is exactly where you are - here and now.

And so I leave you with these words: Embrace this present moment like a gift waiting to be unwrapped. Cherish every second because life is fleeting but its impact can be everlasting if we choose to live fully in each precious moment.

21

Time

Time is a constant companion in our lives, serving both as a friend and a guide. As we navigate our daily routines, it remains ever-present, offering us the moments needed to reflect, grow, and pursue our dreams. In the hustle and bustle of modern life, we sometimes forget just how valuable time can be. It patiently waits for us as we work towards our goals, providing space to learn from our mistakes, adapt our strategies, and make progress. Whether it's the hours spent honing a new skill, the days dedicated to a project, or even the years invested in personal growth, time is always there, reminding us that every small step counts.

Time has a unique way of aligning itself with our aspirations, often revealing opportunities we may not have initially seen. It teaches us that success is rarely instantaneous but unfolds gradually and often requires perseverance. In moments of doubt or frustration, time gently nudges us to keep pushing forward, assuring us that the right moment will come. The beauty of time lies in its ability to transform our experiences, allowing us to appreciate the journey just as much as the destination. As we pursue our ambitions, it is essential to remember that time is not just a measure of how long it takes to achieve our goals; it is an invaluable ally that supports us every step of the way.

In life, time weaves a intricate pattern that is unique to each individual. It is this very pattern that shapes our experiences, molds our character, and determines the course of our existence. Yet, as I delve deeper into the art of perception, I realize that it is not merely the passage of time that defines us; it is how we choose to navigate its currents.

With every passing moment, we are given a choice – to succumb to the whims of fate or to seize control and shape our destinies. Our reactions in times of adversity define us just as much as our triumphs do. It is in these pivotal moments that true character surfaces.

Time Helps us Grow

Investing a significant amount of time and consistent effort into any endeavor can feel daunting, especially when immediate results are not visible. It's easy to become disheartened when the fruits of your labor seem out of reach, but it's essential to recognize that progress often operates beneath the surface. Just as a seed needs time to sprout and grow roots before breaking through the soil, our endeavors often require patience and persistence. The small steps we take, the skills we develop, and the lessons we learn along the way all contribute to a foundation that will support future achievements. Even when it feels like you're treading water, trust that each effort is laying the groundwork for eventual success.

The passage of time can work wonders in ways we might not immediately perceive. Growth is often a gradual process that involves overcoming obstacles and setbacks, which are integral to learning and development. The more time and effort you invest, the more equipped you become to navigate challenges and seize opportunities when they arise. Remember, it's not just about the end goal; it's about the journey and the transformation that occurs along the way. Embrace the process, stay committed, and recognize that every small step forward is a testament to your dedication, even if the results aren't apparent right away.

```
As I sat with my dad one afternoon, he shared with me a
valuable lesson about the power of time."Remember," he said,
"time is a valuable resource that can be used to enhance our
lives and propel us towards success."
```

```
To illustrate his point further, my dad began telling me the
story of the chinese bamboo tree. He explained that when you
plant a bamboo seed, you have to water it consistently for
five years without seeing any visible signs of growth. At
first glance, this might seem disheartening or discouraging.
However, the farmer who plants the seed keeps his faith and
believes in the process, knowing that it will eventually
sprout into a majestic bamboo tree.
And then comes the magical moment when time works its
wonders. Suddenly, after those five long years of patience
and perseverance, the bamboo shoots up with incredible speed
and potential. In just five short weeks, it reaches a
towering height of 90 feet.
But here's what's truly remarkable about this story: even
though it may seem like sudden growth to an outsider's eye,
in reality, it has been steadily growing from the moment it
was planted in the ground five years ago.
```

```
Isn't that incredible? The story of the bamboo tree is like
a metaphor for life itself. It teaches us about
```

```
patience--about persevering through difficult times without
losing hope or giving up on our dreams. It shows us how
essential it is to believe in something greater than
ourselves and to trust in its process.
Just imagine planting that tiny seed and faithfully watering
it day after day, year after year--trusting that something
amazing is happening beneath the surface even when there are
no visible signs of progress. And then finally witnessing
that moment when all your hard work pays off as you witness
rapid growth and transformation. It's a beautiful reminder
that sometimes the most significant changes happen
gradually, even when we can't see them happening.
```

So, the next time you feel discouraged or impatient about your progress in life, just think of the bamboo tree. Remember that your efforts today are like watering your dreams—laying the groundwork for something extraordinary in the future. Keep nurturing those dreams with dedication and unwavering faith, and watch as they grow into something truly magnificent.

Time is an invaluable resource that should not be wasted. Instead of bemoaning moments of downtime or feeling frustrated by a lack of visible progress in our lives, we should embrace these opportunities to improve ourselves. By consistently investing time into our skills and knowledge, we can lay a solid foundation for future success.

The story of the bamboo tree serves as an inspiring metaphor for life's journey—a reminder to have patience and perseverance. Just like the bamboo seed that requires years of consistent watering before sprouting into a magnificent tree within weeks, our efforts today may not yield immediate results but are essential for long-term growth.

So let us remember to keep watering our dreams with dedication and unwavering faith. Let us trust in the process and believe that every moment we invest today will contribute to something extraordinary in our future. With this mindset, we can embrace the power of time and unlock its transformative potential in our lives while it help us grow.

The art of perception lies not only in recognizing this power but also utilizing it wisely to create a life filled with growth, success, and fulfillment.

* * *

Time Heals

Time has a remarkable way of healing wounds and resolving problems. As each moment passes, we find ourselves gradually releasing the burdens of past pain, triumphs, and joys. Our achievements and failures also begin to lose their hold on us, no longer carrying the same weight they once did.

In this process, time creates a gentle space between us and our experiences. It brings harmony and balance into our lives. It has the power to dissolve and dilute our emotional attachments, allowing us to find our rightful place in the grand scheme of things. As a result, our pain is lessened, and our pleasure is tempered. We gain a clearer perspective on our past successes and failures, enabling us to see beyond the realms of love and hate.

So take comfort in the passage of time. It holds the key to healing and growth as it gently guides us towards a brighter future.

> "Time is the greatest equalizer"
>   Krishnna Kode

Time treats everyone equally; it does not discriminate based on wealth or poverty, health or illness, education or lack thereof. It embraces all walks of life with open arms as it dances at the same pace in everyone's life.

My dad always used to mention that how we perceive time can change based on our perspective. It's similar to how when you want a better view; you climb up a hilltop or stand atop a cliff or tall tower. Sometimes by elevating ourselves spiritually we can gain clarity about time and our lives.

When I was younger, I used to believe that time was an enemy—always rushing forward without regard for my desires or plans. But as I've grown older and wiser (or so I'd like to think), I've come to realize that time is not our enemy. It is a companion on the journey of life, guiding us through life.

In moments of pain and heartache, it may feel like time moves too slowly, prolonging our suffering. But as we navigate through the passage of days, weeks, and months, we start to notice subtle shifts within ourselves. The wounds that once felt raw begin to scab over, gradually transforming into scars that remind us of our strength and resilience.

Time allows us to step back from the intensity of our experiences and gain a fresh perspective. It gives us the distance needed to see beyond our emotions. The weight we once assigned to these moments diminishes with each passing day until they become mere memories— lessons learned rather than defining markers of who we are.

Time offers us solace when we need it most, its steady rhythm reminding us that life is a series of ebbs and flows.

Time holds within it an inherent power—an ability to mend what is broken if only we allow it into our lives. It requires patience on our part—a willingness to surrender control.

And so, as we continue our journey through the art of perception, let us not fear the passage of time but instead lean into its gentle embrace. For in its infinite wisdom lies the promise of healing and growth—a brighter future waiting just beyond the horizon.

"You may delay but time will not"
Benjamin Franklin

22

Journey of Life

My dad always had a unique way of explaining complex concepts to me. He often used analogies to make them more relatable and easier to understand. One analogy he frequently shared was that of our lives as passengers on a train journey. He would say, "Imagine our lives as a train journey. This train moves at a steady speed that never changes, just like time."

As the train travels along its path, it stops at different stations. These stations come in various shapes and sizes and offer unique experiences to each passenger on board. Some passengers may find joy and happiness at certain stations, while others might face challenges or difficulties.

The interesting thing is that although the train stops at the same stations for everyone, each passenger's experience is entirely different based on their mindset and perspective. It all comes down to how we choose to see things along this journey called life.

It's crucial to remember that this train we're all on doesn't have a set destination. It keeps moving forward relentlessly, without any pause or respite for anyone or anything. Just like the ticking hands of a clock, time never stops for anyone.

As we continue on this perpetual journey, each one of us will eventually reach our own destination - the end of our time on Earth - or what most people refer to as death. Just like passengers disembarking from a train upon reaching their stop, we too will leave behind this physical existence.

The truth is that we are all moving towards the same final stop at the same speed; however, none of us knows when that stop will come for us individually. It's an uncertainty we all face but tend to forget amidst the hustle and bustle of our day-to-day lives.

Understanding this undeniable truth can help us prioritize what truly matters in life and focus on living a happy and meaningful existence. When confronted with our mortality, it becomes evident that time is our most valuable asset. We must strive to make positive changes in our lives and make the most of our limited time and energy.

Rather than dwelling on trivial matters or getting caught up in material possessions, we should invest our time and energy in building meaningful relationships, pursuing passions, and making a positive impact on the world around us.

Instead of merely being passive passengers on this train called life, we should take charge of the direction we want to go in and make every moment count.

Let's not allow ourselves to be consumed by the monotony of everyday life or become prisoners of routine. Instead, let's embrace each station as an opportunity for growth, learning, and self-discovery. Let's appreciate the beauty that surrounds us at every stop along this remarkable journey.

Remember, you are not alone on this train journey. Each passenger you encounter has their own story to tell and their own battles to fight. Be kind and compassionate towards your fellow travelers as you navigate through life together.

As you sit back in your seat and watch the scenery pass by outside your window, remember that time keeps moving forward relentlessly. Cherish each moment as it comes because once it passes by, it can never be retrieved.

So let us embark on this train journey of life with an open heart and a curious mind. Embrace all the ups and downs that come our way because it is through these experiences that we grow wiser and stronger.

As we continue moving forward on this train called life let's choose love over hate, kindness over cruelty, gratitude over entitlement. Let's make choices today that will leave a lasting impact not only on ourselves but also on those who will board this train long after we have departed from it.

Together let's master the art of perception - seeing beauty where others see drudgery, finding joy in the simplest of moments, and living a life that truly matters.

* * *

Life is a Journey not a Competition

In life, it is easy to become fixated on the idea of winning or achieving a specific end goal. We are constantly striving to be the best, to reach the top, and to come out on top in every aspect of our lives. However, if we take a step back and reflect, we realize that life is not a race with a clear winner. Life is a journey, an ever-evolving process filled with countless experiences and opportunities.

When we view life as a journey rather than a race or destination, we open ourselves up to new perspectives and possibilities. Instead of focusing solely on external achievements or reaching a specific endpoint, we can embrace the present moment and learn from both our triumphs and failures. This mindset allows us to continuously expand our horizons and find joy in our relationships, passions, and personal development.

Success in life is subjective; it means different things to different individuals. It is not solely measured by external accomplishments but also by the joy and fulfillment we find in our own unique journey. As we let go of the notion of winning as the ultimate goal, we can focus instead on cultivating a mindset of continuous improvement and self-discovery.

By embracing this mindset, we become more adaptable to the ever-changing circumstances and challenges that come our way. Life is full of uncertainties—twists and turns that shape us into who we are meant to become. Rather than resisting these changes or trying to control them, let us embrace them wholeheartedly.

The beauty lies not only in reaching an endpoint but also in all the moments leading up to it—the small victories along the way, the lessons learned from failures, and even the unexpected detours that redirect our path. Each experience contributes to us as individuals.

As human beings, it is natural for us to desire stability—to have goals and aspirations that act as guiding lights throughout our journey.

However, it is important to remember that the journey itself is where we find contentment and purpose.

When we let go of the need for a definitive end goal, we become more present in our own lives. We begin to appreciate the little things—the laughter shared with loved ones, the feeling of accomplishment after overcoming a challenge, and the sheer beauty of simply being alive.

Life is not meant to be lived solely for future achievements or for reaching a destination. It is meant to be savored and experienced fully in each passing moment. Every step we take, every decision we make—no matter how big or small—is an integral part of our unique journey.

So let us embrace the uncertainty that life brings us. Let us embrace the process—the ups and downs, twists and turns—that shape us into who we are today. Let us embrace the beauty of the journey itself.

In doing so, we allow ourselves to grow as individuals and find meaning in every experience life has to offer. Our journey becomes an ever-evolving tapestry—a work of art that reflects our resilience, courage, and unwavering spirit.

Art of Perception lies not only in how we view ourselves but also in how we perceive our own unique journeys. By shifting our mindset from winning to embracing, from racing to savoring each step along the way—we unlock a world filled with endless possibilities and boundless growth. May our perception guide us towards embracing the beauty of our individual journeys—one step at a time.

* * *

Embrace the End

Life is a journey, and as we travel through its winding paths, it is easy to become fixated on reaching an ultimate goal. We often believe that there must be a grand destination waiting for us at the end of this incredible journey. However, we must remember that the ultimate destination we all share is death. While this realization may seem daunting, it holds within it a powerful message that can transform our perspective on life.

The awareness of our mortality should not bring us despair or fear; instead, it should ignite a fire within us to make the most out of every precious moment we have been given. The knowledge that our time on this earth is limited can serve as a powerful motivator to embrace every opportunity that comes our way.

Imagine life as an intricate tapestry woven with threads of experiences, relationships, and personal growth. Each thread represents a unique moment or encounter that contributes to the beauty and richness of the whole. When we shift our focus from an end goal to cherishing each thread in its own right, we begin to understand the true essence of living.

It is in these threads where true fulfillment resides - in moments shared with loved ones, in pursuing passions and dreams without hesitation or compromise. By embracing every twist and turn with unwavering determination and an open heart, we allow ourselves to fully experience all that life has to offer.

Embracing the journey means being present in each passing moment - whether they are moments of triumph or moments of struggle. It means finding joy even amidst adversity and seeking opportunities in every challenge faced.

As we navigate through life's uncertainties, let us remember that no journey is without its share of obstacles. It is in these moments of difficulty that we have the chance to evolve. Just as a caterpillar undergoes a transformative process within its cocoon before emerging as a butterfly, we too can emerge from life's trials stronger, wiser, and more resilient.

Furthermore, embracing the journey requires fostering meaningful connections with others along the way. The people we encounter on our path can have a profound impact on our lives - they can teach us valuable lessons, offer support when we need it most, and inspire us to become the best version of ourselves.

Let us not take these connections for granted but rather nurture them with care and compassion. Ultimately, the goal lies not in reaching an external destination but in living a life that is fulfilling and joyful. It lies in leaving behind a legacy built upon love, kindness, and empathy towards others.

We must remember that the ultimate destination is death, we never know for sure when our station will arrive.

So let us embrace this incredible journey called life with open arms. Let us immerse ourselves fully in each moment - the highs and lows alike - knowing that every experience is momentary but shapes who we are becoming.

As we navigate through this intricate tapestry of existence, may we find solace in knowing that our purpose lies not at some distant end point but rather in savoring every experience along the way. For it is through embracing the journey that true fulfillment is found.

23

Swadharma

"I would rather die of passion than of boredom"
Vincent Van Gogh

In our quest to follow the path of dharma, we come across the concept of Swadharma, which essentially translates to "your purpose." It is our natural duty, the most important obligation we have towards ourselves. But how do we identify this purpose? It is not something that can be known right from the beginning, nor can it be guided by others, no matter how well-meaning they may be – not our teachers, parents, siblings, or friends.

Discovering one's Swadharma is a personal and private journey that each of us must undertake on our own. In simpler terms, it can also be referred to as passion or one's true calling.

To identify our individual dharma or true calling, there are certain steps we must take.

Firstly, we need to develop awareness and cultivate an open mind.

This allows us to explore various possibilities and avenues without any preconceived notions or biases.

Secondly, it is crucial to differentiate between role-based responsibilities and duties versus natural duty or true calling.

Role-based duties are those that arise from specific roles we play in life – such as taking care of our family's needs if we are raising a family or fulfilling job responsibilities if we are employed or if you are an entrepreneur you have the duty to manage your businesses and take care of your employees.

However, it is important to note that these role-based duties do not exclude the possibility of them aligning with our true calling.

For instance, someone whose Swadharma lies in caring for their family may find immense fulfillment in doing so. Likewise, an entrepreneur who feels a deep sense of purpose in running their business may also find alignment with their natural duty through their work.

Certain professions come with inherent responsibilities tied directly to one's dharma. Religious priests have a duty to guide followers in matters relating to faith and spirituality. Those involved in charitable causes have the responsibility to care for the people they serve. The list of professions, jobs, and duties is vast and varied, each with its own unique set of responsibilities which are known as dharma.

Dharma, in its broadest sense, refers to the moral law or duty that governs the behavior of individuals and society as a whole. It encompasses universal principles of righteousness, justice, and order that are applicable to everyone. Dharma serves as a guiding force that helps individuals navigate the complexities of life, providing a set of ethical standards that one is expected to uphold, regardless of personal circumstances. It is often associated with the collective good and the responsibilities that come with living in a community.

In contrast, Swadharma is a more personalized interpretation of these principles, focusing on an individual's unique path and responsibilities based on their specific circumstances, calling, and personal experiences. The term "Swa" means "self," and "Dharma" refers to one's duty, thereby highlighting the importance of self-awareness and individual choice in determining what one's duty should be.

In our search for Swadharma, it is essential to remember that discovering our true calling goes beyond societal expectations or external pressures. It requires introspection, self-reflection, and a willingness to embark on a journey of self-discovery.

When we align ourselves with our natural duty – our Swadharma – we experience a profound sense of fulfillment and purpose. Life takes on new meaning as we live in harmony with ourselves and the world around us. Our actions become infused with authenticity and passion, leading us towards a life well-lived.

Ultimately, finding our Swadharma is an ongoing process that evolves as we grow and change. Therefore, it is essential to regularly reassess and realign ourselves with our evolving sense of purpose.

* * *

In our lives, we often find ourselves taking on multiple roles and performing various duties. From being a parent, a spouse, a friend, or an employee, we constantly juggle different responsibilities. However, amidst this chaos of obligations, there are certain activities that come naturally to us. These are the tasks that we excel at effortlessly and enjoy immensely. We become so absorbed in these activities that we lose track of time and never tire of doing them. This is what is known as our true calling or Swadharma.

Our true calling is often referred to as the passion of our life. It goes beyond societal expectations and constraints such as caste, religion, education, or profession. It is not defined by where we come from or what we do; instead, it is an activity that brings us the most satisfaction, happiness, and fulfillment.

Discovering our true calling is a transformative experience. It provides us with a sense of purpose and direction in life. When we engage in our true calling, it feels like second nature to us; it becomes an integral part of who we are.

Imagine being a painter who loses track of time while creating art on canvas or a musician who gets lost in the melody while playing an instrument. These individuals have found their true calling in life through their artistic pursuits.

Identifying our true calling requires self-reflection and introspection. It involves delving deep into ourselves to understand what truly brings us joy and fulfillment. Sometimes it may take years to discover our true passion; other times it may reveal itself unexpectedly.

But once we have identified our true calling, it becomes our duty to ourselves to practice or perform this activity as much as possible. It becomes part of our natural duty in life – the reason why we were brought into this world.

Following one's Swadharma requires dedication and commitment. It may involve making sacrifices and stepping out of our comfort zones.

Society may impose expectations on us, urging us to pursue certain paths based on external factors such as financial stability or societal status. However, if we ignore our true calling and succumb to societal pressures, we risk living a life devoid of purpose and passion.

So It is important to remember that our true calling may not always align with societal norms or expectations. It may require taking unconventional paths or pursuing non-traditional careers.

Each one of us has a unique gift or talent that sets us apart. Our true calling allows us to share this gift with the world and make a meaningful impact on those around us.

Once we have found our Swadharma, it becomes our duty to nurture it and let it flourish in every aspect of our lives.

As we navigate through life, it is crucial not to confuse our role-based duties with our passions. Both are essential elements that require balance in order for us to lead fulfilling lives. Just like the much-talked-about work-life balance, we must also strive to find a duty-passion balance.

Some individuals have managed to integrate their passions into their role-based activities, and these are the people who have truly succeeded. Because by doing so, they are able to find happiness and fulfillment from both their natural duties and their responsibilities within society.

Role-based duties and responsibilities do have limitations, as they are part of collective efforts. We are never fully responsible for someone else's life, whether it be our life partners, parents, children, or even in our business or profession. While we may carry a certain level of responsibility towards them, there is always an invisible limitation that exists if we care to observe it.

However, when it comes to our natural duty towards ourselves - what we call Swadharma or true calling - we hold 100% responsibility. This duty towards ourselves is more important than many of us realize. It is within this realm that we can truly discover who we are meant to be.

Finding our Swadharma requires self-reflection and introspection. It involves understanding our strengths, weaknesses, passions, and desires at a profound level. This deep self-awareness allows us to align ourselves with activities that bring out the best in us and nurture our authentic selves.

Discovering our true calling may not happen overnight; it often takes time and exploration. We must be open-minded and willing to step outside of our comfort zones in order to uncover hidden talents or interests that may lie dormant within us.

Once we have identified our Swadharma – whether it be through artistic expression, entrepreneurship, teaching others or any other avenue – it is essential to cultivate it. This means dedicating time and effort towards honing our skills and knowledge in that particular field. It requires commitment and perseverance to fully develop our potential and make a meaningful impact in our chosen domain.

However, we must remember that Swadharma is not just about personal fulfillment; it also involves serving others. When we find the intersection between our passions and the needs of others, we create a powerful force for change.

Finding balance between our role-based duties and our passions is crucial for leading a fulfilling life. By integrating our natural duties with activities that bring us joy, we can achieve happiness on both personal and societal levels.

As you embark on your journey to uncover your Swadharma, remember that it is never too late to start. Embrace this opportunity for self-discovery with an open mind and heart, knowing that by finding your true calling, you are taking an important step towards living a purposeful life.

* * *

In life, why is it so crucial for us to follow our passion and attend to our true calling? To understand this, we must first delve into the concept of karma.

Karma, in its simplest terms, refers to our past actions and emotions that create residual memories and desires within us. These memories and desires are carried with us as we enter this life, guided by an unfathomable logic and algorithm that determine our exact place, time, and parents.

The purpose behind the circumstances of our birth is to provide us with opportunities to gain the experiences that our soul desires based on our past actions and emotions. By embracing these experiences through the performance of our natural duty or Swadharma, we can attain the very essence of what our soul longs for in this lifetime.

It is crucial to recognize that the only thing that truly matters is the experiences we accumulate during our journey in life. These experiences, along with their resulting memories, are what follow us beyond this physical existence. When we depart from this body, all other aspects become insignificant. We will not remember any relationships forged or places visited nor any achievements or material possessions acquired during our time on Earth because they dissolve into nothingness.

Attending to our true calling brings about immense satisfaction and happiness because it allows us to naturally align ourselves with what we were meant to do in this lifetime. Our true calling transcends societal norms, rules, regulations—what may be perceived by most humans and society at large.

Let's consider an example:

Imagine a wealthy individual earning vast amounts of wealth through their role-based duty but experiencing immense joy whenever they engage in charitable services. Their soul whispers to them that their true calling lies in helping those in need.

Conversely, let us consider a scenario where the roles are reversed. If the individual mentioned above were to find that earning vast amounts of money becomes their natural calling or duty, they can attain inner contentment and true success by dedicating themselves to fulfilling that duty.

In both these instances, we witness the power of true calling—the alignment of our natural inclinations with our daily lives and responsibilities. By blending their role-based duties with their true callings, these individuals can achieve genuine success—a success measured not by external achievements but by the fulfillment of their souls' desires.

Discovering our true calling requires self-reflection and introspection. We must delve deep within ourselves to identify the passions, inclinations, and inner stirrings that resonate most strongly within us.

It might not always align with societal expectations or what others deem as successful or significant. Our true calling is unique to each of us—an individual path that leads us towards ultimate satisfaction and fulfillment.

By embracing our Swadharma, we unlock a profound sense of purpose and meaning in life. We align ourselves with the experiences that our soul yearns for, allowing us to leave this world with a wealth of memories rather than material possessions. Our true calling beckons us towards a life filled with authentic joy and contentment—a life where success is measured by how closely we live in harmony with our deepest selves.

* * *

In this journey of self-discovery, I like the analogy that trying on different outfits while shopping for the perfect outfit is similar to finding our true calling. Each outfit represents a different path, a unique opportunity waiting to be explored. Like the clothes we wear, some paths may fit perfectly while others may feel constricting or ill-fitting.

But how does one discover which path is their true calling?

The journey towards discovering Swadharma requires stepping out of our comfort zones and embracing vulnerability. It means being open to exploring different paths without fear of failure or judgment. It entails venturing into uncharted territories with an insatiable curiosity that would guide us towards self-discovery.

The process itself could be perplexing at times as we grapple with uncertainty and doubt along the way. Yet every step taken outside our comfort zone brings us closer to unraveling the enigma of our true calling. It is a path paved with courage, resilience, and self-belief - qualities that would fortify us against the challenges that lay ahead.

```
I reflect on the immense privilege bestowed upon me - the
freedom to explore and choose my own path. It was a gift
bestowed upon me by my father, who had nurtured my
independence and encouraged me to follow my passions. His
unwavering support had given me not only options but also
free will - an invaluable asset in navigating through life.

I now understand that the path to finding one's true calling
is unique for each individual. It is a personal odyssey that
required self-awareness, introspection, and a willingness to
take risks. It is through this pursuit that we will unlock
our fullest potential and live a life of purpose and
fulfillment.
```

* * *

As humans,we often find ourselves on a perpetual quest to discover our true calling in life. We are driven by a deep desire to find that one thing that truly excites us, ignites our passion, and gives us a sense of purpose. Yet, this journey can sometimes feel like searching for a needle in a haystack, with countless interests and passions pulling us in different directions.

I find myself facing the same dilemma. I am surrounded by various interests and passions but have not yet pinpointed my true calling. It is as if I am standing at a crossroads, unsure which path to take. But rather than feeling discouraged or overwhelmed by these choices, I decided to embrace the uncertainty and step out of my comfort zone.

As I mentioned before I likened this process to trying on different outfits while shopping – each one representing a different passion or interest. Just as we search for that perfect fit when trying on clothes, I am determined to find the path that resonates with my soul.

This journey of self-discovery is not always easy or straightforward. It requires patience and an open mind as we navigate through uncharted territories within ourselves. However, it is also an incredible privilege – one that not everyone has the opportunity to experience.

Our true calling is not about stumbling upon a single passion that defines us for the rest of our lives. Rather, it is an ever-evolving journey that allows us to explore and embrace the multitude of passions that make us who we are.

As we continue on this journey together, let us remember that our true calling may not be found in just one place or one activity but rather within ourselves - waiting patiently for us to uncover its beauty and embrace its power.

And so we march forward, armed with the knowledge that our true calling awaits, ready to be discovered. Let us remember that the art of perception is the key to unlocking our true potential and living a life filled with purpose, passion, and fulfillment.

24

Self-Reflection

Reflecting on our actions, decisions, and experiences is a habit that successful individuals have mastered. It allows them to gain a deeper understanding of themselves, their strengths, weaknesses, and learn from their mistakes. This was a habit my dad picked up from his cousin, Dr. Ravi Babu, during his teenage years, and it has remained an integral part of his life ever since.

My dad firmly believes that self-reflection has helped him gain clarity and navigate life better. Inspired by his example, I have also started incorporating this practice into my daily routine. Every night before bed, I take a moment to ask myself important questions: What went well today? What could I have done better? What did I learn? This simple act of understanding our emotions and actions has proven to be a powerful tool for personal growth and self-improvement.

To truly grasp the importance of reflecting on our actions, decisions, and experiences, let's delve deeper into this concept. When we take the time to pause and think about how our day went, we are engaging in an act of self-assessment. By asking ourselves questions like "What went well today?" or "What could I have done better?", we actively seek to understand our own behavior patterns as well as motivations and thought processes.

This level of self-awareness is crucial for personal growth because it enables us to identify patterns in our lives—both positive and negative—and recognize our strengths and weaknesses more clearly. Moreover, by shining a light on the inner workings of our minds and hearts through reflection, we can navigate life with greater intentionality and clarity. When we reflect on what went well in our day or what could have been improved upon, we are not merely engaging in empty introspection. Instead, we are investing in our own personal development—a pathway towards continuous self-improvement.

Through reflective practices such as journaling, meditation, or simply taking a few moments of quiet contemplation, we allow ourselves the opportunity to learn from our experiences. By acknowledging our successes, we reinforce positive behavior and encourage its continuation. Conversely, by recognizing areas for improvement, we open doors to growth and development.

Self-reflection is not about dwelling on past mistakes or beating ourselves up over perceived failures. It is about gaining insights and understanding that will help us move forward with greater wisdom and purpose. By asking ourselves what we have learned from each experience—whether it be a triumph or a setback—we can extract valuable lessons that will shape our future actions.

Incorporating self-reflection into our daily routine requires commitment and discipline. It may not always be easy or comfortable to confront our own shortcomings or face the consequences of our decisions. However, the rewards far outweigh any temporary discomfort. The more we engage in this practice, the better equipped we become at navigating life's challenges with resilience and grace.

Self-reflection is a fundamental pillar that supports everything I've discussed in this book. It serves as a bridge connecting theory to personal understanding and practical application. When you engage in self-reflection, you're not merely gazing into a mirror; you're diving deep into your thoughts, feelings, and experiences, critically analyzing them to uncover insights about yourself.

This process allows you to identify your strengths and weaknesses, recognize patterns in your behavior, and understand how your past experiences shape your current decisions. By honing this skill, you unlock the ability to internalize the concepts and ideas I've presented in this book, transforming abstract theories into actionable knowledge that resonates with your unique context.

Self-reflection empowers you to navigate through life's challenges with greater clarity and purpose. It encourages a mindset of continuous growth, prompting you to ask essential questions about your motivations, aspirations, and values. This introspective journey not only fosters personal growth but also enhances your ability to empathize with others and understand diverse perspectives. As you become more attuned to your inner self, you will find that the lessons and principles outlined in this book become more relatable and applicable to your life. Ultimately, self-reflection is not just an exercise; it's a vital practice that can lead to profound transformation, helping you to cultivate a deeper connection with yourself and the world around you.

So tonight before you go to bed—or any time you find moments of stillness—take a deep breath and ask yourself: What went well today? What could I have done better? What did I learn? Embrace this act of self-reflection as an investment in your own personal development—a pathway towards unlocking your true potential in life while understanding the art of perception.

Appendix

As you have reached the end of "Art of Perception" I want to take a moment to express my heartfelt gratitude for joining me on this journey. I really hope this book has given you a peek into a new way of looking at things, just like I've been learning and discovering.

Writing this has been a huge part of my journey, and I want to be honest—I'm still learning and growing every day. I'm only 18, and while I've shared what I know and what's been important to me so far, there's so much more to experience and understand. I'm sure my views will keep evolving as I go through life.

I hope you read this with an open heart and a little bit of curiosity. There might be some things I don't quite have figured out yet, but that's all part of the fun, right? We're all on this journey together, and I'm thrilled to share a piece of mine with you.

Thank you so much for reading "Art of Perception" all the way to the end! Your time and attention mean the world to me, and I'm incredibly grateful for the chance to share this journey with you.

I hope you found the book both enjoyable and insightful. Writing it has been a labor of love, and it was my hope to offer something valuable and thought-provoking. Knowing that you've taken the time to read and engage with these ideas is truly amazing.

Thank you for giving my words a chance and for being a part of this adventure. Here's to exploring, growing, and seeing the world through new perspectives.

Sincerely,

Krithi Kode

About the Author

My daughter, Krithi, was born in Chicago in 2005. She is an amalgamation of talents, character, and personality. What can I say about her? She is kind, responsible, intuitive, trustworthy, honest, and intelligent. I take immense pride in the person she has become, as she has grown into the individual I always envisioned her to be. Everything that I tried to teach her, with the little knowledge and experience that I have, she embodied that into her nature and personality. What more could a father possibly wish for in his child?

I have always told her not to compare herself with others, because as a creator, everything she produces is a masterpiece in its own unique way. Whether it's music, a painting, a book, or any other form of artistic expression, her work holds its own value, taking my advice she has started creating freely and boldly without much inhibition.

She started writing this book soon after she graduated from high school happily with a 4.0 GPA. Initially, it started as an essay assigned to her, where I asked her to reflect on everything she had learned from me throughout her life up to that point. As time went on, I encouraged her to delve deeper into each topic and reassured her that she had the potential to be an author. Despite her initial doubts about her writing abilities, she gradually gained confidence with my support and began to believe in herself as she progressed with the project. Now, at just 18 years old, she has proudly established herself as a published author.

She is also an artist who has produced wonderful artworks with brushes and pencils alike. She is a passionate animal lover and has dedicated her time to rescuing both dogs and cats. Additionally she is a passionate reader and has read 85 books in about a year during the COVID pandemic. I really think her reading habit has played a huge role in her ability to write this book. With all those different stories and styles she's absorbed, it's clear that her love for reading has shaped her writing in a big way.

Despite being young, she is wise beyond her years. Her understanding of life is amicable, and she has a good grasp of its nuances. She has eloquently transformed her insights into the chapters of this book.

I hope you all enjoyed reading this book.

Krishnna Kode
  Editor, Publisher

www.ingramcontent.com/pod-product-compliance
Lightning Source LLC
Chambersburg PA
CBHW070858160726
48004CB00003B/1143